Unscripted

Engaging Life Beyond College

Thomas A. Brown

Parson's Porch
Books
Cleveland, TN

Parson's Porch Books

Copyright © 2012 by Thomas A. Brown

ISBN: 978-1-936912-52-0   Softcover

To order additional copies of this book, contact:

Parson's Porch & Company
1-423-475-7308
www.parsonsporch.com

This book is dedicated to my parents A.T. and Doris Brown.
You showed me how to be a guide for the journey.
You have given me love, camp, and so much more.

4

Acts 1

New International Version (NIV)

1 In my former book, Theophilus, I wrote about all that Jesus began to do and to teach 2 until the day he was taken up to heaven, after giving instructions through the Holy Spirit to the apostles he had chosen. 3 After his suffering, he presented himself to them and gave many convincing proofs that he was alive. He appeared to them over a period of forty days and spoke about the kingdom of God. 4 On one occasion, while he was eating with them, he gave them this command: "Do not leave Jerusalem, but wait for the gift my Father promised, which you have heard me speak about. 5 For John baptized with water, but in a few days you will be baptized with the Holy Spirit."

6 Then they gathered around him and asked him, "Lord, are you at this time going to restore the kingdom to Israel?"

7 He said to them: "It is not for you to know the times or dates the Father has set by his own authority. 8 But you will receive power when the Holy Spirit comes on you; and you will be my witnesses in Jerusalem, and in all Judea and Samaria, and to the ends of the earth."

9 After he said this, he was taken up before their very eyes, and a cloud hid him from their sight.

10 They were looking intently up into the sky as he was going, when suddenly two men dressed in white stood beside them. 11 "Men of Galilee," they said, "why do you stand here looking into the sky? This same Jesus, who has been taken from you into heaven, will come back in the same way you have seen him go into heaven."

12 Then the apostles returned to Jerusalem from the hill called the Mount of Olives, a Sabbath day's walk from the city. 13 When they arrived, they went upstairs to the room where they were staying. Those present were Peter, John, James and Andrew; Philip and Thomas, Bartholomew and Matthew; James son of Alphaeus and Simon the Zealot, and Judas son of James. 14 They all joined

together constantly in prayer, along with the women and Mary the mother of Jesus, and with his brothers.

15 In those days Peter stood up among the believers (a group numbering about a hundred and twenty) 16 and said, "Brothers and sisters, the Scripture had to be fulfilled in which the Holy Spirit spoke long ago through David concerning Judas, who served as guide for those who arrested Jesus. 17 He was one of our number and shared in our ministry."

18 (With the payment he received for his wickedness, Judas bought a field; there he fell headlong, his body burst open and all his intestines spilled out. 19 Everyone in Jerusalem heard about this, so they called that field in their language Akeldama, that is, Field of Blood.)

20 "For," said Peter, "it is written in the Book of Psalms:

> "'May his place be deserted; let there be no one to dwell in it,'and, "'May another take his place of leadership.'

21 Therefore it is necessary to choose one of the men who have been with us the whole time the Lord Jesus was living among us, 22 beginning from John's baptism to the time when Jesus was taken up from us. For one of these must become a witness with us of his resurrection."

23 So they nominated two men: Joseph called Barabbas (also known as Justus) and Matthias. 24 Then they prayed, "Lord, you know everyone's heart. Show us which of these two you have chosen 25 to take over this apostolic ministry, which Judas left to go where he belongs." 26 Then they cast lots, and the lot fell to Matthias; so he was added to the eleven apostles.

Preface

In the first year following college I wrecked a car twice, blew out the engine of the same car, began and quit several jobs, lost too much weight, gained too much weight, was cheated on by my girlfriend and didn't end the relationship until she dropped me, was totally pitiful, found my calling, fell in love with one of my former girlfriend's best friends (whom I married), and adopted a dog, among other things. It was quite a year and this list doesn't begin to tell the whole story. All of that happened nearly thirty years ago, yet that year following my graduation has perhaps been the most significant in my entire fifty years. It is not significant for its triumphs but rather for its struggles, challenges, opportunities and all that I learned.

You are preparing to enter your own year(s) following college. In my experience and in the twenty years of experience working with those still in and recently out of college, I have discovered that for many this time period following graduation is often among the most significant times one will live. For the first time you are making choices and decisions that are truly and fully yours to make. Certainly you may have chosen your college or university, you decided a major, and you hopefully chose who would be your significant relationships, but many if not all of these decisions were to some degree influenced by others, especially your family. This influence most often comes in the form of expectations. In completing college you have now fulfilled a significant expectation which has influenced your decisions and choices. You have now or soon will finish a significant portion of what, in this book, I term "the script". Now it is your responsibility, your turn to write your own script for your own life. However there is a problem that commonly emerges following college. You have no idea how to do this; you have not been trained to write your script. Through all your years of education, you have primarily been trained to follow the script that others have given you. Now you are entering the unscripted time of life.

It has been my great privilege and blessing to work with and/or be around students and young adults in one way or another for nearly my entire life. As a child and youth my friends were the counselors and staff at the camps that my parents directed. Then

I found myself journeying through those years myself. Following seminary I directed my own camp where I served as employer, mentor, minister and friend for the students and young adults who worked on my staff. For a few years I focused in youth ministry, but also mentored college interns and followed the youth who were going off to college. Then for the past ten years I have specialized in campus ministry, serving the students here at Appalachian State University in Boone, North Carolina as Presbyterian campus minister. In sharing the journey with these hundreds of wonderful people, I have witnessed, comforted, and guided many through struggles that echo my own challenges in those years during and following college. I have also cheered, coached and celebrated triumphs, accomplishments and discoveries in these same lives. Through each struggle or triumph I have and continue to pray that there will be reflection, learning, growth and the realization of grace.

Several years ago I preached a sermon on a lectionary passage from Acts 1. This passage focuses on the disciples and their journey from the Mount of Olives and the Ascension through the time until Pentecost. In studying the text and preparing the sermon I noted that the journey from the Ascension to Pentecost resonated with my own journey and the journeys of so many students following graduation.

Graduation is certainly a mountain top moment but it quickly becomes clear that though it has been held up as a goal in one way or another for nearly one's entire life, it is a goal that is passed through quickly. Perhaps this is why the term most institutions use for graduation ceremonies is commencement. Read your dictionary, commencement is a beginning point. So through all these years of education your eventual goal has been to reach the point of just getting started. (Frustrating, isn't it?)

In preparing to preach the sermon from this passage, I noticed that in many ways the Ascension of Jesus from the Mount of Olives was like graduation for the disciples. The Ascension was their commencement ceremony, the beginning of their ministry and the task of spreading the gospel.

In looking more closely at the passage, I also noticed that there was a clear transition period between the Ascension and Pentecost. Traditionally this period is another forty day period

8

which in biblical shorthand signifies a significant journey through struggles and opportunities for growth and becoming. Digging deeper I noted that there were six steps or stages through which the disciples passed during this time. They begin on a mountain, pass through a valley, return to a safe place, expand their company, wait prayerfully, and live intentionally. Through these steps they become aware of the Holy Spirit already in their midst and move from clueless to comprehending. I recognized this as a familiar journey. It is a journey that I had travelled myself thirty years ago and one which I have witnessed many times through my years of journeying with students beyond graduation. My sermon was well received. Apparently it resonated with others. I later adapted the concepts into workshop form, which I shared at a Montreat Collegiate Conference in 2009. Now from that sermon and workshop has come this book.

I decided to write a book for the purpose of sharing the insights about this common journey from graduation to what comes next. It is a journey shared by students today, students thirty years ago and apparently students two thousand years ago. I hope that in my exposition and exploration of this journey you might discover a way to not only live through this time of transition but to engage in the struggles and opportunities during this time of your life with more consciousness, awareness, purposefulness, and intentionality. It is in no way my intention to write a how-to-manual or to prescribe a path to follow. Rather my intention is to provide a guide for wakefulness and awareness as you travel your unique path.

However, having walked this way myself and having walked with many others, I have seen patterns and some consistent trends, so I will share the signs of these patterns. You may have a different experience. I have also seen fine opportunities for learning and growth that many have missed. So in the pages that follow I will point towards these in hope that you might be attuned to many of the best opportunities along this journey. Finally, there are points along the way where I will ask you to stop and look around, to take a few moments to reflect on where you are, to note from where you have come, where you are going and perhaps most importantly to notice what is around you at this very moment.

During the years following my own graduation I wrote nearly every night in a journal. I wrote about my experiences, my frustrations, my celebrations, my joys and my pain. These journals are my own testament to the gospel that even in the darkest moments there is a glimmer of light which can be a guide towards better days. These journals were my conscious (occasionally unconscious) wanderings through the desert days of my wilderness years. In the years since, I have been able to revisit those journal entries and to review my steps and missteps. Each time I open the pages and read the ramblings I am able to review what I have learned and how I have grown since those days nearly thirty years ago. In a sense I am able to visit the young man I was and have a conversation with the man I have become. I realize again that I still have so much to learn and have so many ways to grow.

I offer these words that follow as a guide, again not to follow prescribed steps, but rather that you might more consciously take these steps following graduation and write your own script with an open heart, a conscious mind, and an aware spirit. May you relish the journey, the wandering, and the wondering!

Peace –
Tommy Brown
April 30, 2012, Boone, North Carolina

Chapter 1
Wondering *What?*

Then What?

It usually happens during the spring semester of one's junior year. It hits you, "Oh, my gosh, I am actually going to graduate from college in a year!" People start asking *that question.* You know *that question,* "then what?" or "so what are you going to do when you graduate?" These are the warning questions. It is the way those who care about you begin to tell you that it is time to begin to shift gears.

College has hopefully been a great time in your life:

You've had (check all that apply to you) -
- ☐ your mind opened
- ☐ your heart broken
- ☐ your worldview expanded
- ☐ your identity clarified
- ☐ your sleep deprived
- ☐ your certainty questioned
- ☐ your doubts confirmed
- ☐ your body changed
- ☐ your choices narrowed
- ☐ your writing improved
- ☐ your naïveté shelved

And the list could go on and on...

It seems that you spent thirteen years preparing for college and now that you are in the midst of it, or approaching the end of your undergraduate education you feel like you are looking out towards an empty void. In the next year, your last year, it isn't like you are going to have all kinds of time to consider what comes next. After all, the classes keep coming with all of the extra demands of senior projects and senior seminars. You want to make sure you have time with friends, because this is going to be your last fall break, last football season, last spring break, etc.... Then there is the job. Finally you are getting the hours that you need so you can't let that slip. Perhaps there is a girlfriend/boyfriend as well. Relationships! This adds another whole layer to the question, which now sounds like, "So what are you (two) going to do when you graduate?"

Back in that land your parents and/or grandparents call "when I was your age", things must have been different. The script went something like this:

Life – A Play in 5 Acts

Act I –
(scene 1) be born
(scene 2) childhood
(scene 3) get your basic education
(scene 4) graduate from high school

Act II –
(scene 1) get more education
(scene 2) fall in love w/ college sweetheart
(scene 3) graduate college

Act III –
(scene 1) get married
(scene 2) begin a career
(scene 3) buy a house
(scene 4) join a church or synagogue, country club, etc...
(scene 5) have children

Act IV –
(scene 1) continue your career
(scene 2) raise children, celebrate holidays with family
(scene 3) take one or two really great vacations
(scene 4) move up the career ladder

(scene 5) retire

Act V-
(scene 1) travel – move south
(scene 2) visit your grandkids
(scene 3) grow old, play golf and/or bridge
scene 4) die   (the End).

This is the classic script for the American Dream, the one that was followed by the "great American Middle Class" and those who strived to be a part of the middle class for much of the past century at least since World War II and the GI bill. This was the promised life in the Promised Land. When you graduated from college real life began! I know first-hand that of course not everyone followed this script. My father, for one, took a somewhat different course following his military service but he knew what was expected back in the '50s and like most, found his way back to a somewhat standard script.

Needless to say much of this script has been scrapped (except for the being born and dying parts). It has been scrapped, that is, except for Acts I and II. This script basically no longer exists except in the minds of those who were blessed enough to live in a very different time. It seems that the script began to be re-written in the '60s just a generation after it began to be played out on the American stage. Through the '70s and '80s you might be able to recognize the basic plot, though the re-writes that came out of recessions, civil rights, women's rights, gay rights, AIDS, the Vietnam War, globalization, etc... significantly changed the dialogue and drama within Acts III, IV and V. Some scenes became optional others were lengthened, most of Acts III, IV and most of V were removed and replaced with a new Act III and IV that involved multiple career changes and an all too common re-write involving divorce and re-marriage. Somewhere in the '90s and continuing into the current decade, after so many revisions, most of the scenes and acts became optional. From Act III on it seems there is only one word until towards the end of Act V – *IMPROVISE*.

Yet isn't it interesting that though so much of the script has changed or just been scrapped we still mostly follow this same script for Act I and II as if the rest of the play is still the same. One would think that with all the changes in Act III and following, there would be some basic shifts in Acts I & II. But surprisingly there are few. The expectations for you right up through graduation from college remain basically the same. Yet somewhere near the end of Act II, perhaps right where you find yourself now, you begin to look ahead at the script. You start looking ahead for the next scenes, but find that the rest of the script is now mostly unfinished (you know except for that final scene involving death and dying) and again the only direction given is - IMPROVISE.

"What?" You say to yourself, "I've spent all this time in school. Seventeen plus years following directions, learning the script, regurgitating knowledge, and now I'm expected to *improvise?* You've got to be kidding! When is my life going to begin? I've become pretty good at meeting expectations, following directions, reading from the script, even memorizing lines - *but improvising* - that isn't what I've been trained for!"

You are probably right, you have been preparing to follow a script that is at least a half century old. Thomas Friedman, author of *The World is Flat*, and many other cultural observers contend that the predominant educational system in this country remains tethered to the Industrial Age, basically preparing graduates for a world that no longer exists. Friedman contends that in the flattening world in which we now find ourselves, the education system must be transformed and learners, meaning you and me, must be prepared in effect to never really graduate. Our ongoing education will be continuous as we adapt and improvise to keep pace with the technological and cultural transformations of the post-modern world.

Basically improvisation is not an option; it is your reality. improvise/adapt and you also get to choose constantly how to play out the rest of your life. You get to be both the actor and scriptwriter. You get to answer the question "now what" at very regular intervals with very few given expectations for how you proceed from each point forward. Welcome to the paradigm shift that keeps on shifting!

Whose line is it anyway?

Jesus' disciples thought that they knew the script. It was different than yours up to this point, but in some ways, they were just as surprised and taken aback when they came to the end of their second Act.

Here in brief synopsis form is basically what they thought was supposed to happen according to the script that they thought they were following:

Act I -Enter Jesus (promised Messiah) stage left from Nazareth

Act II - As Rabbi he calls disciples to follow him, they follow and he teaches them and prepares them for significant role in his Kingdom (note the capital K)

Act III - As possible Messiah, he preaches/performs miracles, drawing big crowds, thereby making the Romans and Jewish leaders very nervous

Act IV - As crowd confirmed Messiah he makes victorious entrance into Jerusalem thereby affirming his status as the long expected Messiah King of Israel who will lead a revolution against Rome thereby returning Israel to greatness as known under Kings David and Solomon. In addition he would not make the mistakes that David and Solomon made and Israel would be a light to all other nations revealing the justice and righteousness of the God of Israel to all people (In other words this was a great guy to be connected with).

But somewhere just after the start of Act IV, the disciples hear a great unexpected screeching sound, as if the brakes of a car are being slammed and the gears are shifted into reverse. The vehicle abruptly shifts direction and the passengers are flung about by the intense gravitational forces. (I know there weren't cars back then, but it is the best metaphor I can find for how dramatic a shift it must have been for the disciples.) In unison the disciples are heard to say "what the..." Yet we know how the story actually turns out:

> Revised Act IV – As crowd confirmed Messiah, Jesus makes victorious entrance into Jerusalem where he disrupts business at the temple, proclaims a different vision of God's reign, confronts both his enemies and his followers, then is arrested and tried by the Romans, beaten, and killed by crucifixion as a common criminal and disruptor of civil society (not exactly what the disciples saw coming. But wait for what comes next!)

> New Act V - After three days Jesus rises from the dead, appears to Mary and other women, then appears to the twelve disciples, and for the next forty days continues to appear to the disciples re-interpreting (in light of recent developments) all he has taught.

> New Act VI – *Enter Jesus and the disciples somewhere on the outskirts of Jerusalem on the Mount of Olives...*

This is where we join the disciples and where all those willing to journey in their Christian faith eventually join the disciples. It is the place where they and we go from following the script to "making it up as we go along". This is where we go from journeying in certainty to walking in faithfulness. This is where it all becomes IMPROVISATION.

In Luke's book *The Acts of the Apostles* this is what he says happened:

Acts 1: 6-11

Then they gathered around him and asked him, "Lord, are you at this time going to restore the kingdom to Israel?"

He said to them: "It is not for you to know the times or dates the Father has set by his own authority. But you will receive power when the Holy Spirit comes on you; and you will be my witnesses in Jerusalem, and in all Judea and Samaria, and to the ends of the earth."

After he said this, he was taken up before their very eyes, and a cloud hid him from their sight.

They were looking intently up into the sky as he was going, when suddenly two men dressed in white stood beside them. "Men of Galilee," they said, "why do you stand here looking into the sky? This same Jesus, who has been taken from you into heaven, will come back in the same way you have seen him go into heaven."

Notice what the disciples are asking about. They want nothing more than to get back on script. "Lord, are you at this time going to restore the kingdom to Israel?" In other words "take the lead. We're ready to keep on following you. You're the director. Our next line is... .? Whenever you're ready... .?"

Doesn't it sometimes seem that life would be easier if we just had a script and a schedule to follow? If at every moment the next steps and the timing of those steps were clear and certain? This must be what so many people seem to be looking for as they look for and seem to find "certainty". In this scenario, certainty would be giving someone or something else the authority to write your script; to tell you how to live, to give you all the right answers, to make everything clear. Many people seek to turn their script over to other authorities. The authorities may be church leaders, or scripture, or a parent, or a partner, or a nation, or greed, or lust, the list of gods goes on and on. But there on the Mount of Olives, and here in our own lives, we are eventually faced with the fact that the next steps are ours to take. Trusting in God's goodness and authority alone, this same God who chooses in love to let us write

17

our own script, we are given the chance to improvise and create our own next steps in our own timing. You know, the whole free-will thing.

Isn't it interesting that Jesus raises the issue of authority in his response to these disciples when he says, "*It is not for you to know the times or dates that the Father has set by his own authority.*"

The disciples were seeking certainty. They wanted the script not only for now but for eternity. Jesus responded with what Presbyterians would attribute as an affirmation of God's sovereignty. In other words, he says God does know with certainty the time and place for what has been, what is, and what will be; that is not for us to know. To paraphrase a Barack Obama line from a few years back "that is beyond your pay grade". At this point, Jesus assumes the role of Rabbi/Teacher as always. "Students, one last time, God loves you so much that he gave you me. Because of what I have done you are free to take the next steps in faith. You won't necessarily know what the future holds but you know that God holds the future. The future therefore is free for you to improvise. Knowing that the God of Love, the God of Grace, the God who stands here in your midst is not going to play tricks on you. God is not going to trip you up. Nor is God going to turn back on God's word. So you trust, have faith, believe and take the next steps. You are free to improvise, create and take your time."

On his CD *Songs and Stories Live*, Singer/Songwriter David Wilcox weaves a story around his song "Hold it Up to the Light" from his earlier CD *Big Horizon*. In his story Wilcox talks about how through the years since he first wrote the song he has come to the realization that God is not some sort of game show host trying to trick us if we choose the wrong door, take the wrong step, follow the wrong path. In life we can eventually learn that there isn't a wrong door, or step, or path. Some paths might be more difficult and/or adventurous but not necessarily "wrong". I recommend that you go to davidwilcox.com and listen to the song from either CD. This way you get the full impact of David's wonderful songwriting and performing. (Go ahead. I'll wait.)

At some point it finally takes moving down the mountain and stepping out faith that God is not going to let you miss the life for which you have been created. Despite what so many say about God, that isn't God's game. There isn't a trap door, except for those of our own fearful imaginings.

The disciples had yet to comprehend how Jesus had changed the game. He simplified and clarified the rules of the game. He said "Love God with all your heart, soul, mind, and strength and love your neighbor as you love yourself."

It would take the disciples awhile to begin to comprehend and become more comfortable with improvisation. Here before he ascends to heaven, in his last words to the disciples Jesus reminds them of their prompt "to be my witnesses".

If you have ever done "improvisation" in a theatre class then you may remember that you are always offered a prompt or set-up of the scenario you are to improvise. For example:

- *A family of four heading out on a long vacation – go...*
- *Two old men in a fishing boat – go...*
- *A pastor walking into Sunday service late – go...*

From these brief prompts the actors are free to improvise action and dialogue. The "performance" is not rehearsed; it is not always smooth, but it is often creative, engaging, and often funny and/or touching. Drew Carey's show "*Whose Line Is It Anyway*", comedy troupes such as Second City, and performers like Robin Williams base their acts in the art of improvisation, performing without a script with only a prompt.

Before ascending to heaven Jesus reminds his disciples of their prompt from which they are to improvise:

- *Be my witnesses – go... .*

This prompt is still in effect for those of us who would call themselves disciples of Jesus. Yet Jesus doesn't just provide the prompt, he also sets the stage and provides the audience for the "improvisational performance" of the disciples. "... *you will be my witnesses in Jerusalem, in all Judea and Samaria, and to the ends of the earth".* In show business terms the disciples were going to open their show in Jerusalem, then take it out on the road for an unlimited run in Judea (this for their Jewish audience), and Samaria (for their not-so-Jewish audience) and then on the World Tour for anyone who would come and "see the show".

Finally, or actually first, Jesus reminds the disciples that they will have all they need to improvise, to witness, to go *Unscripted.* Not only have they spent three years with him, but soon they will have access to the Holy Spirit. They will have all they need to do this in trust, in faith, and in love. Jesus says " *But you will receive power when the Holy Spirit comes upon you... "*

The Holy Spirit is generally the least understood, least comprehended, and least acknowledged figures of the doctrinal trinity (except perhaps in Pentecostal branches of the Christian Faith). In William P. Young's novel of an encounter with the Trinity, *The Shack,* the figure of the Holy Spirit is imaged as a woman. She is a figure of inspiration, creativity, imagination, and beauty, but yet hard to really see fully. Young's protagonist Mack first encounters her like this:

> *"As she stepped back, Mack found himself involuntarily squinting in her direction, as if doing so would allow his eyes to see her better. But strangely, he still had a difficult time focusing on her; she seemed almost to shimmer in the light and her hair blew in all directions even though there was hardly a breeze. It was almost easier to see her out of the corner of his eye than it was to look at her directly."*
> *(pg.* 84 - *The Shack)*

If one asks an actor, artist, or a musician to clearly identify where or what is their inspiration, their creativity, their muse, they are often unable to specifically name an event, a person, or an experience. Many say inspiration comes from a vague, elusive something just out of focus. In the same way, the Spirit of God can be accessed by those who open themselves to this mysterious possibility. The Spirit seems to be difficult to identify and seems just out of sight.

For the disciples this Spirit would come to them visibly like "flames", like "breath" on the day of Pentecost. This would be the inspiration and the power that they would come to depend on as they improvised their next steps of discipleship. Yet at this point, on that mountaintop they would not even begin to comprehend Jesus' words.

Watch out for the Men in white coats

In Luke's telling, *"After he said this, he was taken up before their very eyes, and a cloud hid him from their sight."* Their Rabbi, their Teacher, their Lord was no longer visible to them in the physical form that he had been and in whatever form this had been for the last forty days. Figuratively speaking this was the Disciples' graduation ceremony. On that mountaintop they spoke to their teacher for one last time, they listened to one last lesson. Then garbed in his robes Jesus "went home" and they stood there looking up.

I remember my own graduation from College and I have seen many graduation ceremonies since. In all the academic regalia the professors and administrators march in, speeches are offered, awards are given, and degrees conferred. Finally as *Pomp and Circumstance* plays, the faculty exits out of sight, you may get one last chance to speak to one or another, perhaps those who have been special mentors and/or friends. You have graduated and the roles have changed. It is clearly time for next steps and a new direction.

Graduation ceremonies are not generally a time for humor (that is unless everyone in your class is handing the college president marbles, true story) yet there on the Mount of Olives is found what I consider one of the funniest scenes in scripture. They were looking intently up into the sky as he was going, when suddenly two men dressed in white stood beside them. *"Men of Galilee,"* they said, *"why do you stand here looking into the sky? This same Jesus, who has been taken from you into heaven, will come back in the same way you have seen him go into heaven."* Do you get the humor? The disciples have journeyed with Jesus for three years, they have heard all that he has spoken, and they have witnessed his death, his resurrection, and now his ascension. They have been given their prompt and a promised inspiration. Yet they stand there looking up to the sky apparently towards heaven. You've got to love these guys!

21

I think this seems even funnier when you consider the visual. Here we have a group of men standing on a mountaintop just staring up towards heaven. Have you ever played the game where you stand in the middle of a crowded place and point up at something just to see how many people will look up towards what you are pointing? Eventually someone will ask "what are you looking at?" In this case we have two men in white robes (think white coats) asking them, "What are you looking at? Why do you stand here looking up towards heaven?"

These disciples, like so many through the ages of the Christian faith and even still today, stand around looking up towards their imagined heaven. Just when Jesus has just told them to go, to act, to witness, there they stand looking up. Within Christian and other religions is the field of *eschatology* that concerns itself with end times, the apocalypse, heaven and hell, etc.... . Among the movements studied in eschatology is Darbyism. In the nineteenth century an Irishman by the name of John Nelson Darby drew from various mythologies, literature, interpretations of apocalyptic Judeo-Christian scriptures, and his own creative imagination to develop a detailed system that became known as Dispensationalism. Darby came to North America in the 1860s and 70s spreading his "end times" message in the midst of Civil War and Reconstruction. Needless to say, in that period many seemed to be looking for an explanation for the strife and turmoil of the present age and Darby's image of "darkest before the dawn" seemed to resonate. It resonated especially in a time that seemed confusing and uncertain. Darbyism or Dispensationalism became an important component of what has been expressed in the twentieth and current century as Christian Fundamentalism. This is just one among several "Christian" movements that focus on eschatology, standing there looking up towards an ancient image of heaven in the three level creation and asking the question that the disciples asked Jesus "Is this the time?" They also commonly interpret the signs of the times and make the pronouncement "The time has come or is coming soon!"

This "escape hatch" theology where God comes in and rescues everyone like me from all those who are not like me has been destructive and distracting to the core message of the Christian faith. If it is where you are I implore you to consider the implications of this line of thought. If you are curious and would like to dig into eschatology and its expressions through history then do your research and navigate a variety of perspectives.

If Jesus' response wasn't clear enough when he said "It is not for you to know the time and place" then certainly it should have become clearer when the two men in the white robes come and say "What are you doing?" and then nudge the disciples on their way strongly implying "GO and DO". Finally the disciples get it and abruptly shift their focus back to the here and now. (There's that screeching car once again.)

How's Life?

There are two questions that I tend to ask the college students with whom I am blessed to work. The first is "how's life or how are you doing" by which I am checking in on how things are going in the here and now. Usually the response is a basic "okay" or "good" or "great" or "fine" which then leads me to ask "What's 'okay' or 'good' or 'great' or 'fine'?" This is when I get to listen to stories about relationships or lack thereof, about roommate issues, about course expectations, about parent expectations or issues, about stories from the weekend or a party or an evening. This is when I get to ask more questions about choices and decisions. This is when I'm asked for guidance about this issue or another.

The other question which I tend to ask is "what are your plans for... the weekend, spring break, the summer, next semester or (the biggie) after you graduate?" I try to reserve the deeper versions of this question for times when the student and I can really have a chance to talk. Though sometimes I will just throw it out there to remind them that they need to be thinking about what's ahead and perhaps give them a chance to think about it so we'll have something to talk about when I see them next. Also I don't just save the *summer, next semester* or *after you graduate* questions for juniors and seniors. These are questions that I'll offer to all students.

I have been teaching some form of First Year or Freshman Seminar Course for the last eight years. Two assignments that I have required in each of these classes reflect these two questions. The first written assignment I give each semester is to have the students write "Their Story" in other words "how's life". Through this assignment I find out something about each student, their back story, and some of their thoughts and feelings in their new reality as college students. Towards the end each semester I assign a future scenario paper "your life in 5, 10, 15 years" in other words "what are your plans?"

Through my years in campus ministry and teaching, students have responded to these formal and informal questions in a variety of ways. I've worked with students who are very intentional in all that they do and have thought through their lives for the next 5, 10, or even 15 years. They know exactly why they are attending college, why they chose their major, who they are going to marry, how many children they plan to have, and have set goals for their career vocationally. They have their script written out in clear detail. These students are the exceptions. For the most part the responses to my assignments or questions tend to be much less specific. Even when considering the next five years, with few exceptions students tend to follow the generally expected script. You know the one that is left over from the '50s and '60s, the same script that their parents intended to follow. My sense, however, is that most of my students haven't really given the future, even as far as the coming summer, very much thought. They are in college, they have followed the script successfully thus far, and they seem to be counting on the fact that the script will always be there for them to follow.

This "american dream" script is so standardized and imprinted in our unconscious that we tend not to consider other options. I am not generally concerned for most students as I read their papers, for they seem to have some improvisational awareness built into their "plans". I am however concerned for many other students who fall into three categories.

I am concerned for those who have over-planned and/or over committed to one script, plan or dream for their life. They have *written in* their spouse, their children and their career. Their plan is to advance steadily up the ladder until they retire; visit

24

grand-children perhaps travel overseas and then die. I am equally concerned for those who seem to walk through life unconscious and clueless, passively waiting for life to happen to them. Many of these students might be on a *treadmill path*, perceived to be caught in an inescapable catch-22 life that they may or may not come to question during an eventual mid-life crisis. Finally, I am concerned for those who (like me after college) seem willing to give up all of their personal dreams and visions to follow someone else's script for them. This someone else may be a parent, a boyfriend or girlfriend, or anyone else who they will do anything to please.

Many of the college students I encounter on a daily basis, like the disciples, seem to be headed for a screeching abrupt surprise. This surprise is not a bad thing, the lessons can be helpful, but these lessons can be and often are painful. My prayer is that this pain does not result in *so much* disappointment, disillusionment, and disheartenment that it becomes a future impediment or blockage for their seeing and seizing opportunities. My prayer is that they will be able to find support and resources that will enable them to begin to write their own script (thus this book.)

A Resource to Consider: Futuring Scenarios

It may seem like a contradiction that I have written about just stepping out in faith and improvising yet now I write about how I ask students about their plans for the future. In my classes and in my conversations with students I often explain and help students employ a futuring methodology that I learned in seminary in a very helpful course utilizing Edward Cornish's book *The Study of the Future: An Introduction to the Art and Science of Understanding and Shaping Tomorrow's World.* This methodology is based on developing future scenarios along a continuum from *Best*, to *Status Quo*, to *Worst Case*.

Very briefly this futuring methodology begins with trend analysis. Trend analysis is simply a means of examining a current trajectory or path that something or someone is currently on. For example: one might consider cultural trends, political trends, sales trends, or personal trends or trajectories. The next step is to consider various change factors. Change factors are events, elements, or intentions that can possibly interrupt and/or redirect a specific trend or trajectory. For example: a significant change factor in our national trajectory was the events on 9/11 and following. Another example of a change factor on a personal level might be a break-up in a relationship with a significant other. These change factors can be either internal (those upon which we have influence) or external (those upon which we have little or no influence) or both. Again for example: an internal change factor in a personal trajectory is marriage. An example of an external change factor would be a hurricane which destroys one's home. In each case change is going to happen. Within each moment and/or period of change whether internal/external/or both there is opportunity to impact trajectory. In other words; it is at such points that choices and decisions whether personal, communal, national, or universal can impact the trajectory or trend lines that emerge from the period of transition resulting from a change factor.

Perhaps a visual will be helpful:

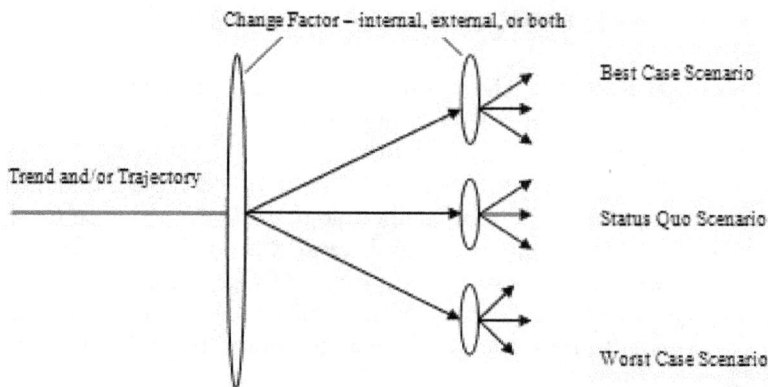

Change Factor – internal, external, or both

Best Case Scenario

Trend and/or Trajectory

Status Quo Scenario

Worst Case Scenario

As you can see in this diagram, choices and decisions can result in a new trend line/trajectory towards best case, status quo, or worst case scenario. This is what I mean by improvisation and/or writing our own script. It is at this point that with appropriate reflection, self-awareness, and awareness of external

26

and internal factors that one can improvise appropriately and/or adapt appropriately and thereby influence the trajectory or trending towards the best case scenarios (which is what I assume most people desire and that according to Judeo-Christian scripture God desires for creation. Deut. 6 "That it may be well with you".) External change factors certainly happen, i.e. the current/recent recession, but we can respond and make choices and decisions even within these transitional periods that can influence the course of our personal, communal, national, and/or universal trajectory.

Here are visual samples of one global and one personal futuring scenario:

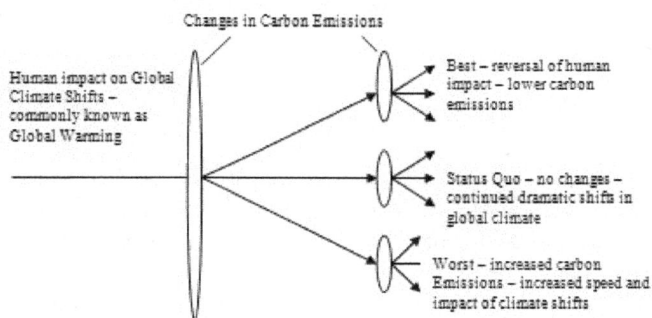

Changes in Carbon Emissions

Human impact on Global Climate Shifts – commonly known as Global Warming

Best – reversal of human impact – lower carbon emissions

Status Quo – no changes – continued dramatic shifts in global climate

Worst – increased carbon Emissions – increased speed and impact of climate shifts

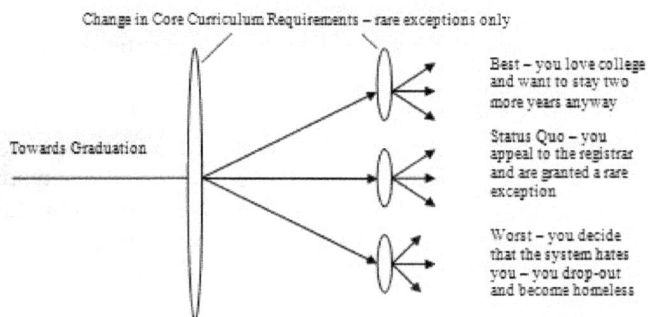

Change in Core Curriculum Requirements – rare exceptions only

Towards Graduation

Best – you love college and want to stay two more years anyway

Status Quo – you appeal to the registrar and are granted a rare exception

Worst – you decide that the system hates you – you drop-out and become homeless

I do encourage students to consider their futures and therefore their planning at least as far as an awareness of best case, status quo, and/or worse case scenarios is concerned. I encourage them and encourage you to do this planning, because even though I have faith in a loving God who desires that it may be well for us, we each have choice and free-will. Among those choices is to passively receive what the world throws our way or to actively respond and influence as much as possible the course that our lives take.

Graduation

For nearly twenty years you have been consciously preparing for the moment when you get to make the choices, the decisions that will mean something for you and for others. You have been waiting to move beyond the preparation stage, the education stage and begin to apply all this knowledge you have accumulated. You have been waiting to assert yourself as an adult and to make your way in the world.

Congratulations you are going to graduate. The time of transition has begun. Go ahead, take one last look towards heaven and perhaps say a prayer. But don't linger too long because there are these two figures coming your way dressed in white. Maybe they are angels or perhaps a couple of nice young aides from a nearby mental institution. Either way they will be curious about what you are looking towards and what you are waiting for. They will helpfully remind you that this mountaintop is only a temporary destination. Your life and your calling are down in the valleys.

So there is your what. What are you waiting for?
You're going to get off this mountain. You're going to start writing your own script. You're going to improvise and adapt – *a lot*. You're going to stop looking up and step out in faith. You're going to hold it up to the light and trust in God's goodness. You're going to be alright.
So what are you waiting for?
Move along now.

Chapter 2
Wondering *Where?*

Walking through graveyards – the Kidron Valley

Between the Mount of Olives and the walls of Jerusalem lies the Kidron Valley. In Jewish tradition this was the place where Elijah would return and where the Messiah would first be seen. In Christian tradition it is through this valley that Jesus, his disciples and other followers processed on Palm Sunday. When one visits Jerusalem even today, as I did in April of 2001, you are struck by the fact that the Kidron Valley seems filled with graves and tombs. It has been tradition since before the time of Jesus to be buried in the Kidron so that when the Messiah returns one can be among the first to be raised from the dead.

In our story, on the day when Jesus ascended to heaven, leaving the disciples standing, gaping towards heaven, the first thing they did (upon somewhat getting their wits about them) was to walk through the Kidron Valley back towards Jerusalem. In Acts Luke simply says, *"Then the apostles returned to Jerusalem from the hill called the Mount of Olives, a Sabbath day's walk from the city."* The shortest path from the Mount of Olives to the traditional location of the Upper Room is directly through the Kidron Valley, walking directly through this extensive graveyard.

I don't know if you have ever spent much time wandering around in graveyards. It is actually among my favorite things to do. I may be weird. Even a few years ago when traveling with my family on a Caribbean cruise I found myself walking through graveyards in various Caribbean towns examining the gravestones and wondering about the lives of the people buried below my feet. When I lived in Louisville, Kentucky I would often take guests and even my youth group at Highland Presbyterian Church for walks through Cave Hill Cemetery. Cave Hill is a beautiful old cemetery

29

that features among other famous headstones the one and only Colonel Sanders of KFC fame. It was a great place to do a church school class on or just after Easter.

In literature and mythology graveyards are places of revelation, of quiet, of contemplation. Consider Hamlet and "poor Yorick" as young Hamlet comes to terms with mortality even in jest. Poets, artists, writers and musicians have throughout the ages found inspiration among the tombstones for works both macabre and enlightening.

In our contemporary culture we seem to seek a distance from death and therefore it seems odd to simply walk among gravestones. It is no longer common for graveyards to be placed in the center of town and certainly not in suburbia. Only older churches may still be surrounded by graveyards. More recent churches now sometimes feature a columbarium off to one corner of the property with nice neat niches and plaques. Death itself has been seemingly shoved aside as we now neatly tuck it away on the outskirts of town, rarely passing by, and even more rarely walking through the midst of it.

Yet this is what the disciples did as they came down from the mountaintop returning to life as they thought they had known it. It seems they had sought to stay on the mountaintop because of course that is where Jesus would return. We would all like to live on a mountaintop and not in the valleys. Yet it is in the valleys where, of course, we and the disciples encounter the stark reality of humanity's mortality – death as can only be realized and regarded in graveyard.

A Moment on Mountaintops

My parents were church camp directors. The very environment in which I was raised, beautiful wooded land, a flowing river, campfires, seemingly ever present community, etc... was for many a "mountaintop". It was a place "set-apart" for retreat and renewal. Then my college, Maryville College, was within constant view of the Great Smoky Mountains. I even married a woman from Asheville, North Carolina, another mountain community. Now at this point in my life I am blessed to live in Boone in the North Carolina High Country. All of these places are for many places for retreat, for retirement, and/or places to aspire to visit or to live. Living in such places and in such environments I have learned to appreciate some of the lessons in scripture about mountaintops.

In this story from Acts it seems that the disciples would have been content to stay on the mountaintop and await Jesus' return. In another story from Matthew's gospel we find Jesus, Peter, James and John on another mountaintop. On this lofty peak Jesus is "transfigured", standing in stark light with Moses and Elijah. There on the Mount of Transfiguration, Peter wants to build tabernacles or booths there on the mountain and just stay. However, Jesus admonishes Peter and the others that they must come down from the mountaintop with him. He also adds the mysterious restriction that the vision and the insight that they have seen is for them and is not to be shared at this time. Throughout various sacred texts including the Judeo-Christian scriptures, mountaintops are places where the divine is encountered, where revelations are given, where visions are sought, and where retreats are taken. In these scripture stories, mountain tops are sacred spaces, set apart, and not meant for the profane living of the day to day.

Whenever people visit Boone, North Carolina in the summer or fall they will often find themselves up on a mountaintop gazing at the wonderful vistas. Sometimes you might hear them say, "I wish I could live right here, build a house right on this spot, and wake up every morning with this view." There are many (too many) who have in effect done just this, building homes on mountaintops, up on or near the peaks of the Blue Ridge. It isn't until winter comes that they discover various aspects of their folly. When the winter winds blow (it is not unusual to have 65 mph sustained winds and gusts exceeding 100 mph throughout the winter), then the snows come (average snowfall above 4500 feet is 60+ inches), and you have to drive down steep ice covered roads to the village in the valley for food and supplies. After a few weeks of winter (which can last well into April at these elevations) the wisdom of building on the mountaintop generally comes into question. This is why native people and early settlers knew that life was to be lived and sustenance harvested not upon the mountaintops but rather down

31

in the valleys. It is in the valleys where life, real life, can be lived and sustained.

I have learned in my own life that when one lives day to day to day upon a mountaintop, at a wonderful camp and conference center or in a beautiful location such as Boone, North Carolina one discovers that even mountaintops can become figurative flatlands or hills or valleys. Even in such beautiful sacred places life can become profane, ordinary, common, or even dark and dull. Life is not lived on mountaintops. Life is lived fully in the ups and downs, in the places between, in both the bright open vistas and in the enclosed dark spaces. Mountaintops are great places to visit, but even when you live there they too can become valleys. C'est la vie - such is life.

Life, Death, and all that

Back in our story, the disciples are given a bit of a shove down the mountain, "what are you looking at?" and they find themselves in a graveyard. Can you imagine the thoughts and conversation as they walked?

> *"Let's get this straight. Jesus isn't coming back immediately? We're not going to raise an army and battle those who had him killed?"*

> *"We're supposed to go wait. Wait for this Holy Spirit thing... ."*

> *"Now I get it. Let's see, we followed, he died and then came back to life, now he is gone again, and we're going to start telling others about what has just happened."*

> *"Oh look! We're in a graveyard! No big surprise there!"*

It isn't that the disciples were stupid; it is that they were so much like you and me. Or to be more specific, that they are like those of us who hang on to the seeming comfort of certainty. In their certain focused way of being human, they were so wrapped up in their clarity (as I talked about in Chapter 1) and in their win-

32

lose, black-white, dualistic understanding of how the world operates that they were struggling to perceive things in light of Jesus' revelation and interpretation of how things really are in the reign of God. They were also being perhaps stereo-typically male. After all, the group we're working with was exclusively male, at least up to this point in the story.

I highlight that they were men in the midst of this struggle because it seems that men especially have more difficulty changing mind and heart and therefore soul. This is not to say that women have a much easier time of it, but for various reasons of which I do not have space to get into, women tend to have minds, hearts, and therefore souls that can, at least a bit more easily be changed and can hence perceive and receive transformed realities. It was the women who we are told first encountered the risen Christ at the tomb and quickly proceeded to spread the gospel. The men on the other hand had to see Jesus again and again and again and still it seems they struggled to comprehend what they saw.

If this was the case for these men of the first century, who we assume had not yet completely succumbed to platonic duality, then you can see why it is that much more difficult for our minds trained in modern certainty to understand the complexity and multiplicity of such concepts as "loving one's neighbor" or "the meek shall inherit the earth". Especially males, but even a majority of female modern minds have been fed a steady diet of dualism, of either/or-ness, of us/them, of win-lose, of my success means someone else must fail, etc.... Perhaps this is why western modernity has tried so hard to put everything in neat little boxes, even death and especially God. Led by the male of the species, our boxes bring the illusion of order to the seeming chaos of creation. We make it labeled, ordered, named, and tamed. We mount our stack of boxes and stand securely and certainly at the highest point. We place ourselves and our kind in the place of dominion there at the peak, on the mountaintop, of the ordering and categorizing of our own understanding of creation.

Among the hopes arising from the transformative times that we find ourselves in (and perhaps that you who are reading this book might personally find yourselves in) is that this might be a time of shattering and shuffling our deluded perspectives. Specifically the shattering of the illusion that you or I or anyone sits on top of the created order or can by our own understanding or means really find order, security, or certainty in anything. Our current age has been given (labeled as we remain in the habit) the term "Post-modern". It really doesn't describe very much except for what it is not. All we can discern from this term is that we have somehow moved beyond the modern era. There are shelves and files filled with texts and terabytes of data dedicated to post-modernity.

In very brief summary it seems that we are in a time where the illusions of certainty and of order and clarity that were so enshrined in the modern era have been shattered. In other words, written here already, the script has been scrapped. What is true and certain depends upon one's perspective. Therefore all is relevant and life is adaptation and improvisation.

We find ourselves in a transitional time globally, culturally, and perhaps personally. You may disagree, but I find this very hopeful and exciting. It is in such times when the hard shell of certainty has been fragmented that we human beings, even the male of the species, historically have become open to change and to a new perception of reality. Many are frightened in such a time of change, so frightened that they will fight to the death (to many deaths) for their certainty. Thus we have witnessed the recent rise of radical religious fundamentalism. These people are so frightened that they will terrorize others to assert their perceived and certain understanding of reality. If challenged, which is what post modernity is doing, they will hold on with all their often corrupt and assumed power to stay on top of the ordered and named towers they have constructed. In his own time Jesus knew this and named this. He was killed for doing so.

One of the ways we might perceive the time we find ourselves in the midst of is that of a cosmic liminal space. Liminal space is undefined time. It is neither this nor that. It is between times. Think of dusk or dawn which is neither day nor night but rather some of both. Think of the spring or fall equinox, which is neither summer nor winter. Think of graveyards, which is where the living go to visit or be with the dead. These are all liminal spaces.

I love it that the first place that the disciples find themselves following Jesus' ascension is in the liminal or between space of the Kidron Valley. Here amidst the tombs and the gravestones, the disciples have the opportunity to reflect upon life and death. They can consider Jesus, who they are perhaps beginning to comprehend is somewhere in between. They perhaps begin to glimpse that this Jesus is one who is breaking the boundaries that were generally assumed to be unbreakable. What was once certain is not so anymore.

I also imagine that the disciples were reflecting upon their own lives. Reflecting on the twisting course their lives had taken in the last few years and of the dramatic and screeching turn of the last forty-some days. As they walk past the tombs they perhaps recognize a few of the more famous figures from the history of their people. They see the graves of kings, prophets and priests. Then the questions come tumbling forth:

> *"All of these are waiting for the Messiah to return. If Jesus is the Messiah, are they still entombed or are some of these graves empty? If they still wait, then is Jesus really the Messiah or were the rabbis mistaken in their interpretations? If the rabbis are mistaken in their interpretation, then what else might they have missed or have misinterpreted?"*

> *If Jesus is who Jesus is... then???"*

There are so many questions with no clear answers. With no clear answers the illusions of certainty come crashing to the ground.

This simple riddle is and has always been the trouble with belief systems based on certainty. It is a house of cards. If you remove one of the cards, then the whole structure tumbles down and one is left without belief. One is left at least for a time with only questions.

If - then? Now - what? Again and again the questions come. These questions still arise when we have little choice but to walk through real or metaphorical graveyards. These questions arise when we have little choice but to encounter some sort of death, the death of certainty or perhaps the death of our beliefs.

Eventually the question comes, now what? It is at this point that we enter the grace of liminal space.

It is not unusual for the questions that come to be tinged or coated with anger, sarcasm or cynicism. People you had trusted, systems you had counted on, beliefs you had balanced were all lies! Remember when you were young and you were finally told the truth about Santa Claus? Did you get angry or did you get even? You know the pre-teen eye-rolling or cynical smirk. These adults are not to be trusted; after all there was that multi-year fabrication about Santa, the Easter Bunny, and Tooth Fairy. "You can't believe anything they say and they continue to pull this crap on my little brother and expect me to play along."

That was your first conscious cognitive stage shift. You have hopefully been through a few stage shifts since then and in each one there is a sense of loss and therefore the accompanying denial, anger, bargaining, sadness, and acceptance. These feelings and this process expresses itself in various ways in various people and some people become stuck at a point in the process. However, most will move on and adapt to this new cognitive space in which they now find themselves functioning. But there has been loss and we need to make space for the process and flow of grief.

At such times and in such moments we need to allow ourselves to grieve what has been lost whether real or conceptual. In her book *Mudhouse Sabbath*, Lauren Winner describes how Christianity (and therefore the majority of western culture) no longer grieves well. She writes,

"We lack a ritual for the long and tiring process that is sorrow and loss. A friend of mine (Lauren's) whose husband recently died put it like this: 'For about two weeks the church was really the church – really awesomely, wonderfully the church. Everyone came to the house, baked casseroles, and carried Kleenex. But then the two weeks ended, and so did the consolation calls.'"

Lauren goes on to describe the orthodox Jewish ritual process of Avelut, which last for a full year, and then annually acknowledged process of mourning. It is a process that accompanies the mourner, gives space to the mourner, and then holds the mourner within community calling the mourner back to life while acknowledging the ongoing nature and years of grieving.

This scenario involves actual death, the loss of a loved one. This is important, but so is metaphorical loss. Yet, imagine how little attention is given to metaphorical loss, the loss of certainty, the loss of beliefs, and the loss of all that we had come to depend upon.

In the case of Orthodox Judaism, as in many ancient traditions and cultures, many passages are still acknowledged and ritualized. It is acknowledged and encouraged that persons must be allowed to enter liminal space, allowed to enter sacred space, between space. Through ritual and in time the person is encouraged, guided and allowed to feel, to grieve, to struggle, and therefore to grow and to emerge changed, transformed. Upon emerging there is a feast and a celebration in the community which welcomes the new person into the ongoing life of the community.

We retain some elements of these rituals in Western Christian contemporary culture; baptism, confirmation, marriage, funerals. For the most part these rituals are completed, done decently and orderly, and then conveniently placed back into their box. This is our personal and cultural loss, for it is in such liminal time, space, and ritual that we can allow ourselves to be shattered to our cores. It is in such times, consciously but more often unconsciously, when we let go of our certain constructs and illusions and we step down from the perches created, formed, and defended by our egos. It is then that we finally open ourselves to God, because at last there is nothing else. This is when we can move from just belief and begin to enter into a trusting relationship based on faith, based on the gritty reality of our simple, beautiful, and humble humanity.

Father Richard Rohr has spent a great deal of his writing and speaking on this topic of liminal space and time, especially in his male initiation and rites of passage work. Summarizing (and perhaps interpreting Rohr) he says that such space and time is necessary for growth and change. For without such times of struggle, without such experiences of uncertainty, then our egos will never be open to God or the other. There will be no hope for the intimacy for which we are created.

Struggle and doubt are important times in our lives. Such times are not to be wasted.

So how am I doing so far?

As I have already said, among the things about graveyards is that they have a tendency (if one allows it to happen) to cause us to reflect upon not only death but also upon life. Specifically graveyards might spark reflection upon one's life to date. I hope that just reading this statement might start you on a mental journey back through your life and through your life's story. Go ahead, take a moment and reflect on your life up to this very moment.

What do you remember?

What are the marker moments, the change factors, and the growth steps?

What are the memorable points in your story, those that lead from one chapter to the next?

Go ahead, I'll wait.

Notice that it probably isn't the day to day points that most easily come to mind. More often than not it is the transition moments, the change points, the marker moments. Throughout your life there have been and there will continue to be periods of transitions. Already you have gone through the changes of puberty, you have probably moved homes and/or schools, perhaps you have gone through significant changes in your family of origin, perhaps you have had someone close to you die (if not human, then animal). You have had formed and broken relationships including friendships and romances.

Each change, each transition represents a significant marker in your life story thus far. It is at these points when telling your story you might say something like "and then I... " It is at these points where the story shifts and a new chapter begins. You are or will soon be at such a marker; graduation from college. That makes this a significant moment. Take the time therefore to pay attention.

When you really take the time to look back and consider in retrospect you might be able to see how you responded to the various change factors you encountered either internal or external. You can consider the choices you made or were made for you in your youth and how these choices impacted the track of your life, your life story. These are the points which are shown in the futuring scenario diagrams as the convex lens shaped object. It is at such points we might enter liminal space and make choices and decisions and emerge on a different path, changed/transformed:

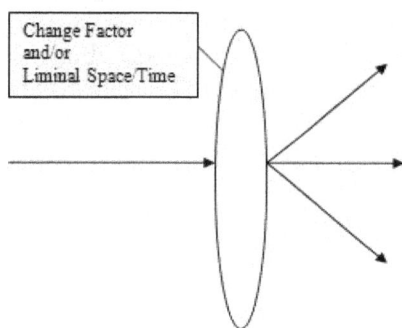

Change Factor
and/or
Liminal Space/Time

Take a few more moments to consider the following questions concerning transitional periods in your own life:

- At various transitions did you ease through the transition or did you fight it?
- In response to the transition did you become more of your real self or did you struggle to remain just the same?
- Were you conscious of the choices and decisions you were making in response to the changes and challenges you faced at each point of transition?
- How might a fuller consciousness and/or awareness of the transition and its potential impact have changed your responses, your choices, your decisions?
- Who helped you with your various choices or decisions?
- Who helped you through your various transitions?
- Did you take time to grieve or even acknowledge loss?
- At what points did your choices and decisions move you towards best case, status quo, or worst case outcomes?

What I am asking you to do with these questions is to look back upon your life and to consciously evaluate how the choices and decisions you made in certain critical periods played themselves out in the course of your life. Through such an exercise in retrospect you might begin to develop an increased consciousness and/or awareness in regards to how you enter and move through such moments in your life. Such as the moment you are either entering and/or approaching called graduation. I am not implying that you are unconscious at the moment, but that it is possible for all of us to become more deeply conscious and aware throughout our daily lives. Such depth of consciousness and awareness can be immensely valuable in these critical transitional junctures. A deeper consciousness might influence the choices and decisions we make and even who we consult and include during such times.

The process of consciously working one's way through decisions, choices, and responses in life's transitional moments are known in Christian terms as *periods of discernment*. There are still periods of discernment for those passages in life that are still acknowledged in Western Christian culture such as baptism, confirmation, marriage, and death. Typically each of these rituals or rites is preceded by a guided process of consideration and reflection for those making decisions. Pastors visit parents prior to infant baptism, those preparing for confirmation are offered and sometimes required to participate in some type of class, engaged couples meet at least once with a minister prior to the marriage ceremony, and family members meet with ministers and/or funeral directors to determine the rituals around death and dying.

Another typical period of discernment in many Christian denominations is some type of structured process that is required prior to pastoral ordination. In such a process it is common for a person who is considering a vocational calling to ministry to be required to meet with committees on local and regional church governing body levels through a multi-year process.

In a broader sense a similar process of discernment is common in other fields as well, though it may be structured as licensing requirements, an apprenticeship, or internship. Each process provides an opportunity for conscious reflection and conversation regarding vocational decisions, challenges, learning

40

and growth. In such periods one is perhaps provided a mentor and/or supervisor to help maximize the learning opportunities of such periods.

In western culture these periods and processes are common for career and/or vocational discernment. Perhaps you participated in some form of discernment process as you were choosing which colleges or universities to apply. Perhaps you were given some vocational discernment or career assessment tools during high school through your guidance counselor. You might have already taken advantage of the resources offered through your current school's Advising, Peer Career and/or Career Placement Office. All of this can be very valuable in helping you through your decisions, choices and vocational discernment.

Yet as I have hopefully made clear, it is much less common in our western culture (especially outside of religious cultures) to attend to and provide support for other significant periods of discernment. For example, how many are provided an opportunity to participate in an internship or offered an assessment tool for full participation in sexual activity? Did you have a celebration or ritual when you received your driver's license? Are there requirements or mentoring offered before becoming a fully licensed parent? What are the available assessment tools and or apprenticeship programs available for entering a committed non-marriage relationship? What about job loss or transitions? Not even religious communities tend to recognize these moments. Are there common rituals for leaving one community and entering a new community? I could go on and on.

To be fair there are good resources available and training programs for most of the transitional moments mentioned. There are resources available for most facets of relationships, parenting, and becoming sexually active (often they are in the self-help section of bookstores and come with titles such as _____ *for Dummies*). However, utilization of these resources and tools is not common and certainly not required. Nor do I believe that they necessarily should be. What I am advocating for is personal conscious discernment during such periods. I am advocating for you to be more aware and conscious, not only in regards to career

41

and vocation, but in all of life's significant stages and transitional moments. I especially and specifically encourage you to do so in the one you are now entering.

So, how are you doing so far? How's life? Consciously speaking?

A Sabbath Walk

Before moving on, I want to look at one more elements from the passage from Acts. Luke describes the distance that the disciples walked from the Mount of Olives to either the Upper Room or another location in Jerusalem as "a Sabbath Day's journey away". First of all, for those needing facts, a Sabbath Day's Journey was the distance which was prescribed by rabbinic tradition and therefore Jewish law as an allowable distance for orthodox observers to walk on the Sabbath. Scholars who delve into such things determine that around the time of Jesus and the disciples, this distance would have been in the 6000 ft. range or approximately 1 mile. Okay, the facts are covered.

I am more intrigued by the concept of a Sabbath journey or a Sabbath walk. For this moves us to the metaphorical level, and being an English major, this is where I am always drawn to go. Think about Sabbath and the spiritual practice of Sabbath keeping. Again, in *Mudhouse Sabbath*, Lauren Winner (who for a period of her life was an Orthodox Jew) writes,

"I remember that, for Jews, the Sabbath shapes all the rhythms of calendar and time, the entire week points toward Shabbat. The rabbis, who are always interested in the subtleties of Torah prose, puzzled over the two different versions of the Sabbath commandment. Why in Exodus, does God tell us to remember the Sabbath, whereas in Deuteronomy He instructs observance of the Sabbath? One story the rabbis tell about the difference has to do with ordering time. Sunday, Monday, and Tuesday are caught up in remembering the preceding Shabbat, while Wednesday through Friday are devoted to preparing for the next Shabbat."

What Lauren is describing is a deep consciousness and awareness of God and God's intimate involvement and modeling of human life that comes from developing and following such spiritual practices as Sabbath keeping. Therefore on a Sabbath Day's walk or journey one must then be especially conscious and

42

aware of God and God's intimate involvement in human life. On that day, needless to say, the disciples must have been SO very conscious and aware of GOD.

Wait a moment. I think I might sense some cynicism among my readers. Come on Tommy, all this about graveyards, liminal space, processes of grief and loss, consciousness and awareness, who has time for all that? I am graduating here! I am busy looking for jobs, keeping the folks off my case, and just trying to have a little fun. Who has time to be conscious?

Taking care of the basics

It would be great if during these transitional moments, these periods of discernment, you could just hang out and have conversations with friends, with family, and with those whose opinions you respect and wish to consider deeply. In order to really sit down and talk with the people you would like and to collect those opinions and guidance, this often requires travel...
and travel requires a vehicle
and vehicles require fuel
and you require fuel too
and purchasing fuel for you and the vehicle requires funds
and attaining funds either requires going to parental units
and/or having a paying job
and having a paying job takes time
and having a paying job requires being clean sometimes
and having a paying job requires getting some sleep
and getting sleep and being clean requires a place to live
and having a place to live requires funds
and/or additional acquiescence to the parental units
and all of this requires more funds
and more funds requires more of a job
and more of a job requires (more often than not) requires
        transportation
and transportation often means a vehicle
and... fairly soon you find yourself in a never ending loop of
        requirement and expectations.

43

Fairly soon the only time you have for any kind of real discernment is between all the other things that are requiring so much of your focus and attention. Before you know it life is *happening to you* and you have had very little say in the direction that it is taking. You are neither following a script nor intentionally improvising one for yourself. If you are not careful, aware and conscious then these unconscious improvisations can become your life. Perhaps this is not the life that you really want, but rather a life that you might suddenly notice (note consciousness) and find (note awareness) yourself living. I'm hoping that the last thing you want is for your life, this life that God has blessed you with, is for it to be perceived as a trap – a classic catch-22.

(If however, you are content with life just happening to you without your having a conscious say in what happens, and you have read this far, put the book down. You are wasting your time. Go back to your unconscious, unintentional life.)

By the way there are some religious communities out there that just love looking up towards heaven, while they wait for Jesus to come back and do it all... Life happens in unconscious, unengaged, uninteresting (in my opinion) bliss. La, la, la... .

For those of you are who are still reading, I do acknowledge that it is necessary to take care of the basics. While in the midst of an intentional conscious discernment process you do need to take care of the basics of life. Jesus was apparently strong enough to venture into the wilderness for forty days of discernment. During this time, according to tradition and text, he fasted, taking in only the basics necessary for survival. There are many other stories throughout human history of individuals who chose a deeply ascetic approach to deep discernment and deep vision. Consider John the Baptist, the Apostle Paul, the Buddha, various prophets, desert fathers, Thoreau, Tolstoy, and more recently the story of Christopher McCandless who inspired John Krakauer's book and Sean Penn's film *Into the Wild*. This choice of physical and relational denial can be a path to deep discernment and I imagine a deeply spiritual experience. However, nature has taught me that there various channels of differing depth within the same river. In the same way, there are various channels of spiritual journeying. One may flow deep and quick, while another may flow shallow and slow, eventually all the water gets to the same waterfall. Even that water which momentarily gets stuck in an eddy.

The trick I think for most of us is how we dynamically balance taking care of the basics – job, housing, transportation, food, etc... while taking time for intentional discernment. In my own experience following college, though I struggled to do so, I was eventually able to find a job which allowed me to sustain the basics of my life. Finally getting this job, I made the space and the time to spend with those who guided me and helped me locate a discernible course. With so many of the young adults I have worked with it has required them letting go of one script they had written for themself, again taking a job which meets needs, while beginning a process of discerning a new script, which eventually takes them into the next chapter of their story.

Remember that even as the disciples were walking through the graveyards of the Kidron Valley that no matter how dark, deep, and disorienting their encounter with death, life, and uncertainty became they continued to walk. They continued on, making a "Sabbath Day's journey" back to a place they knew. It was a place where they would be surrounded by friends and companions, a place where a meal was probably prepared and waiting, a place where they could eventually sleep and dream. Traditionally they would return to this same place, The Upper Room, where just a few weeks ago they had according to the Gospels gathered together at a meal, celebrated the Passover and had heard these challenging words, "Do this in remembrance of me". All their basics were covered, and then some... .

Of course I don't know exactly where you will find yourself following graduation from college. Perhaps it is what you hope will be a brief move back home, or perhaps a longer stay back home. Perhaps you will stay in the town and even the same apartment where you spent your senior year. Maybe you are going to another college for grad school in a few months. Perhaps you are set-up in an internship that provides housing. Perhaps you are heading out in your car with friends into the great unknown. Wherever you find yourself in the next few months, I pray you will find yourself in a place where you have enough of the basics covered so you can take time to make the most of this liminal space in which you find yourself. *Don't waste good liminal space.*

So there is your *where.* Got it? Good. Let's move on.

46

Chapter 3
Wondering *Who?*

Friends are Family

Among the many things that require some major getting accustomed to once you graduate from college is not having friends around almost all of the time. This may actually be kind of nice or perhaps kind of weird depending on your experience and disposition. It is so simple while at college. You're ready to go hang out with some friends and all you have to do is walk down the hallway or text someone or arrange something on Facebook. There is almost always someone to do something. Even when you are studying in the library, or walking from or to class you can almost always count on running into someone that would be cool to hang. Someone is almost always around even sometimes when you would like some self-time.

This easy accessibility changes once you graduate. Sure you may still have a group of folks who you can count on, but all of you now must be intentional about making plans and coordinating your schedules. It seems that what was once so simple, just getting together to just hang out, has now become complicated.

I am in no way saying that after you graduate you will no longer have friends and you will be alone forever (tears begin to fall). I am saying that a fairly common experience for post undergraduates is that creating, keeping and maintaining friendships, especially deep friendships, takes more effort than it ever did during high school or college. The social opportunities are just not the same as they have been during college. Even when one opts for graduate school, the demands of academics, work, and living situations change. You will also have changed and perhaps some of your former friends are still living like they are undergrads. They may be stuck or worse. You are moving on or at least trying to move on. You probably don't ever want to live in a dorm or even on campus ever again (though if you consider it that was a great way to connect with and make friends). After college you want your own place. If you have a roommate she/he is often someone else in similar circumstances rather than an especially close friend. Another post-college factor that you will discover is that it now takes much more effort to find potential healthy romantic relationships. You could always do the bar scene – but I said "healthy".

One of the things that happen following graduation is that these friends with whom you have spent the last four-plus years tend to go off in lots of different directions. Suddenly all six of your closest friends are spread throughout the globe and not just for a summer but for the foreseeable future.

You keep in regular touch via Facebook, e-mails, and an occasional phone call or Skype, but it has gone from daily conversations to weekly at best. You coordinate your schedules and manage to get together for a week at the beach and maybe some weekends back at school for football games. But something always comes up for a few friends who aren't able to make it that weekend. Then the weddings or the serious relationships begin.... You start getting invited to be in this wedding party, and then another, and then another. It seems all your friends from college are getting married or in serious commitments and you can't even get a date much less meet someone that you even really want to date. Now your close friend has a new partner and/or is planning a wedding or surprisingly already married (when did that happen?). It seems that this is all she ever talks about. You want to hang out with just your buds for the weekend, but two of them can't because one is checking out caterers with his fiancé and another is tied up doing something with his new in-laws.

This never happened back in school!

If you are still in college, you should talk with someone who has graduated in the last few years. Ask them what they miss most about college and I bet that nine out of ten of them will say something about missing their friends. It is simply more difficult to create the kind of relationships you have during college once you graduate. I'm not saying it is impossible, but that it just requires more intent and effort. It requires more effort to make

48

new friends and it requires more effort to maintain current friendships. Sounds like fun doesn't it?

This complication with friendships happens at a time and in a phase of your life when close, deep, honest, open friendships are perhaps more important than ever before. This happens at a time when you need your friends to talk with, to cry with, to laugh with, and to discern with. You need them more than ever and they seem not to be available. It isn't that they don't love you (I don't think), or that they don't care for you in the same way as they did in college, it is just that they are otherwise engaged. Either they are literally "engaged" and/or traveling, working, or just simply overwhelmed with their own adjustments to post college realities.

Your friends would love to be there for you to talk, to listen, to play, or just hang, "*but tonight is not a good one can you call back on Thursday?*" To be honest you may resent this some, after all there was that time in your junior year when you were working on a project and he/she came in your room crying their eyes out. You put away your computer and stayed up with them until 3:00 a.m. talking it through. Then you had to get up at 6:00 a.m. and piece together your project, such as it was, for the presentation in your 9:00 a.m. course. She/he cost you at least a letter grade in that class and now they are too busy to talk with you tonight when you need her/him and when you just REALLY NEED TO TALK!!!? Arrrrghhhhh!!!!!!

So you sit alone thinking about who else you can talk with tonight. Hmmmmm. You visualize each possibility on your mental list. One is on the west coast and is probably still at work, another is in Spain, another is in a serious relationship and is probably "otherwise engaged" and the list goes on. You could wait and talk with your roommate when she comes in from work but that isn't until after 11:00 p.m. You need to be up at 7:00 a.m. for your own job. So you open up your laptop to see who might be on-line. Which one of your friends might be available at this moment? Got to love technology! This works. Your friend in the "serious" relationship is home alone tonight as well, so after a few IMs back and forth you decide it is better to talk on the phone. He was really wondering how you were doing... .

All this is to say that you should try not to take any of your friends for granted. You are going to need them someday soon. Now is the time to nurture those relationships. If you haven't already done so, take the risk and have some of those deep, down & dirty, honest, revealing conversations that will lay the foundation for a late night call sometime in the near future. It is actually best to take that risk with several of your friends and best if with some of them are of the opposite sex or sexual orientation. You are going to need multiple perspectives to really consider for the decisions you will be making in the next few years. Go ahead, I encourage you to take the risk and open up. Tell your real story, without the embellishments (okay just a few) and do some revealing. It may feel like you are getting naked and in a figurative (perhaps literal) sense you will be. You are becoming vulnerable, but it will be worth it on one of those long late nights sometime in the next few years. Make the investment, take the chance. You can also invite the same from them. I guarantee that it will pay off, for these will be the friends who will be there, if at all possible, further on down the line.

One of the current shows on TV that I have enjoyed is *How I Met Your Mother* on CBS. This show is the most successful recent incarnation in the line of *Friends*. Not only are these shows funny, well performed and creatively written, but they are relatively based on the relationships which occur during this post college young adulthood. Television situation comedies have always used "family" as their primary vehicle. In the 1950s and early 60s the "family" was nearly always a nuclear family. Think *Leave it to Beaver, I Love Lucy, Father Knows Best*. As the "script" of what is meant by "family" began to change in the late '60s, television began to reflect this shift. Consider *The Courtship of Eddie's Father, Gilligan's Island*, even *The Andy Griffith Show*. Then in the '70s & '80s *MASH, Sanford and Son, Different Strokes*, and *Cheers* among so many others presented or reflected a variety of images of "family". Now family was not only those people you lived with, your nuclear family or in therapeutic terms, one's family of origin, but now you could choose your "family". Along with all the other choices and options in contemporary life, choosing your "family" becomes another choice of adulthood and of course we all want to be "where everyone knows your name". The imagery of what is meant by "family" had shifted. But it wasn't until *Friends* in the '90s that a show focused so clearly on the unique dynamic of twenty-something relationships.

This dynamic has been explored in such books as *A Tribe Apart: A Journey into the Heart of American Adolescence* by Patricia Hersch. More recently the topic is addressed in an excellent resource for congregations considering their ministry with young adults, *Tribal Church: Ministering to the Missing Generation* by Carol Howard-Merritt. In her introduction Howard-Merritt writes, *"Among a new generation, "tribe" has become a term for a subculture, a network of relationships, or a group of people who care for each other in the most basic ways."* Through the book she suggests ways how the traditional "tribe" of a congregation can become truly welcoming for the "tribes" of young adults with among other things their non-traditional definitions of what is meant by "family".

One of the key dynamics that is witnessed and celebrated in these shows such as *Friends, How I Met Your Mother,* and also in Broadway musical expressions of twenty-something tribalism *RENT,* is the concept of "fidelity". In these shows the core group of friends sticks together through all their various situations, struggles, challenges, and changes. Jobs, lovers, cars, apartments, even family of origin may come and go but (to use a not nearly so cool reference) "friends are friends forever", at least during the run of the show.

From author/seminary professor, Kenda Cresy-Dean, I have learned that in the past the key question for young people was a question of meaning, 'Will my life have meaning and purpose?' For more recent generations this question has changed. The key question of life is now one of fidelity, 'Will you be there for me no matter what?' Creasy-Dean in her book *The Godbearing Life* and in subsequent books and lectures explores how the church has so often missed the questions of both youth and young adults and therefore missed the opportunities for ministry. When they have been seeking fidelity which is found in authentic relationships, congregations have given them programs and an inconsistent and regularly burned-out parade of youth and young adult interns and/or what end up as short term relationships.

51

I talk about and reference church because it is what I know. But the parallels are consistent throughout our culture. You who are young adults seek fidelity in authentic relationships and we give you temporary part-time positions with an every changing parade of associate managers and supervisors. You seek mentor guides who might provide wisdom, leadership and insight, but culture offers ethical miscreants who parade as political and religious models of the worst of adolescent behavior. Is it any wonder that you find yourselves unsure in committed adult relationships and therefore seek sexual release in casual "hookups"?

Among my prayers for you as you transition from college into what comes next is that you be conscious of the importance of your friends. I pray that you will find a way to carry some of your friends along with you one way or another. I pray that despite the difficulty once you have left the "friend rich environment of college life" that you manage to find new friends as well and that you will have a group of friends who will have fidelity and who will "be there for you no matter what".

Anam Cara/Soul Friends

Consider, once again, the disciples' story in the first Chapter of Acts. Let me first provide a reminder of the back story. These twelve (whoops!) now eleven disciples named here as *Peter, and John, and James, and Andrew, Philip and Thomas, Bartholomew and Matthew, James son of Alphaeus, and Simon the Zealot, and Judas son of James,* had basically been traveling and learning together for three years. They had come from different backgrounds and experiences as diverse as tax collector (who had worked on behalf of the Roman authorities who had arrested, tortured and killed zealots) and a zealot (who probably had at one time threatened the life and/or killed tax collectors.) Needless to say there were probably some very interesting group dynamics through the time they spent with Jesus.

Among my roles at Appalachian State University, I teach a recreation management course called *Leadership and Group Dynamics.* In this course we explore how all groups move through a common developmental flow. Among the theories is *Tuckman's five stages of group development. The five stages are forming, norming, storming, performing, de-forming or adjourning.* Storming is the conflict stage that all groups eventually move through as they work out how they will best function.

We get some glimpses of this "storming" among the disciples throughout the gospels. For example: *"Who sits at the right hand of Jesus?"and "Get behind me Satan."* Jesus speaks at length in John's Gospel about his hopes for the disciples being One, just as he and the Father are One. Like any group of people it is easy to imagine (if we allow them to be real) that the disciples were taken through a deeply intimate group development process. By the time they accompany Jesus into Jerusalem, witness his crucifixion, share in his resurrection, and after forty days ascend and descend Mount Olivet; I imagine that this group and the others who waited their return back at the upstairs room had become a very tight group. They had been through their share of storms, literally and figuratively, and had remained faithful, loyal, and committed to their purpose (or their purpose as they could comprehend).

As I closed the last chapter, I noted that this group, the disciples, knew that they had friends, that they had a place, and that they had the basics covered. Therefore though they were moving through the Kidron and passing through the valley of questions, the valley of death, each one and together knew that they could find comfort, support, and rest there with "family" in the Upper Room. Luke writes in verse 13 of Acts, *"When they arrived (in the city), they went upstairs to the room where they were staying"* and then he names each of the eleven disciples.

Have you ever wondered about the arrangements that had been made for this "upstairs room"? According to various gospel passages well over forty days before the part of the story we are working with, this upstairs room had been reserved for use by this group of Jesus and his followers for their traditional Passover Meal. Then as their leader was arrested, sentenced, and crucified, the Upstairs Room became their refuge and their hiding place in the city. Following a very confusing Sunday morning it then became the Jerusalem location for various re-appearances, gatherings and what I imagine to be spontaneous general hoopla. Now it was once again a refuge, a sanctuary and where they would gather and wait for what Jesus had called the "Holy Spirit".

My guess is that they had an open ended arrangement with the owner of this establishment. The room had gone from being a banquet hall to safe room to meeting room and now "church". It became the location for the gathering of the "tribe".

This reminds me of one of the quirks about the TV shows that I mentioned earlier. Did you ever notice that in all of these shows about "friends as family" it is very clear that there is a special public place for gathering? In *Cheers* there is the bar, in *Friends* there is the coffeehouse, in *Seinfeld* there is the diner, and in *How I met your Mother* there is the booth at the bar. Here in the Gospels and Acts there is the Upstairs Room. In the gathering of the "family", in the gathering of the "tribe" these places become sacred space, ritual space, sanctuary, church. In contemporary anthropological terminology these are known as *Third Places*. Neither home nor work, the Third Place is where social interaction and community happens.

Think about the special gathering places for you and your friends throughout college. Where will your *Third Place* be after you graduate from college?

For the disciples returning to the Upstairs Room meant not only returning to what had become their Third Place, but it also meant returning to a larger group of friends and family. Scholars acknowledge and the scriptures indicate fairly clearly that the group that is traditionally known as eleven male disciples actually consisted of a larger group of Jesus' followers including a fair number of women. This is referenced in the passage from Acts 1 when Luke writes in verse 14, *"They all joined together constantly in prayer, along with the women and Mary the mother of Jesus, and with his brothers."* I will work with specifics in this verse in later in this chapter and in coming chapters. For now I simply want to note that the group included women, other men, and Mary the Mother of Jesus. Important to note is that beyond a diversity of interests and experiences, this group of friends also included gender and generational diversity.

Imagine the stories and questions as they entered the space that day. They found a snack of dates, took a drink of wine, and then responded to the questions of the others:

54

" Where is Jesus? "Did you see him?"
"Is he going to be here for dinner?"
"Dinner? Well... you know Jesus"

Once again, these friends have had a shared experience like few others. Again referencing group dynamics theory, we learn that one of the things that brings a group of people close together is shared experience, the more intense the experience, often the more intense the bonding. Many approaches to group dynamics are based on this factor. If you need a group to bond and learn to depend on one another, then remove them from their comfort zone, their everyday, and have them encounter challenges that they must work together to overcome. Consider group initiative courses, high ropes, and other adventure based experiential education methodologies. This concept also plays out among the participants in camp programs, trip & travel adventures, and mission trips. Yet all these are usually fairly controlled circumstances. In extreme survival situations, such as military combat, hostage situations, or natural disasters, groups and individuals can form very intimate bonds that may even be stronger than the bond between members of the same family of origin. In such extreme situations, these bonds are on such a deep and intimate level that they are difficult to describe. (Perhaps Jesus referenced this when he spoke, *"who is my mother, who is my brother... ").* Over time a marriage partnership will, if given the chance, evolve into just such a deeply bonded relationship. As a couple in this partnership together they have overcome obstacles and survived extreme challenges.

I imagine that the bond among the disciples was probably of this extremely intimate type. They had certainly shared some very intense common experiences. I also imagine that this is exactly what Jesus intended. In the Celtic spiritual tradition, these types of friendships/relationships are given the name in Gaelic *A nam Cara* which is often translated in English as *Soul Friend.* These are the deep, trusting, authentic relationships in which you have shared stories, experiences, challenges, adventures, pain and struggle. These are the friendships within which you can be brutally honest and securely take risks. These are the relationships that have lasted through the years, through the changes, through the journeys up the mountaintops and down through some pretty deep dark valleys. This is the type of relationship, the type of friendship that I imagine Jesus had with his disciples and that he sought to nurture among those who followed him.

I am blessed to have several Anam Cara in my own life. My wife Karen is a soul friend as well as a wonderful partner, lover, and companion. Karen and I have been married for over 25 years. We have grown together on this deep level, on a soul friend level, as we have struggled with ourselves, with one another, and with the challenges that life has put before us. We have also shared much joy as we have partnered in raising our sons Hayden and Shafer and in creating a home that is welcoming and open for our friends and family. I could go on and on, but suffice it to say, Karen is my Anam Cara and my wife.

Another soul friend is my college roommate Bryan McFarland. He and I met during my freshman year of college and have since shared a great variety of experiences and adventures. He was best man in my wedding and Karen & I "eloped" with he and his wife Diane when they married and where I performed the ceremony while Karen was the lone witness. We have attended seminary together, traveled together, led conferences together, written songs together, commiserated about the church together, and etc., etc., etc.... . Our stories are deeply intertwined.

Then there is Gavin Meek, another of my Anam Cara. He, Bryan, and I were in seminary together. Following seminary, I directed the camp and retreat center for Louisville Presbytery and Gavin was pastor at a very supportive congregation in Lebanon, Kentucky. There are many ways we began to strengthen our friendship but among the most significant moments happened when one of the youth in Gavin's church who was also on my staff at camp, a young man named of Lebron Gaither, was tragically and senselessly murdered. Gavin called me and invited me to join him and we shared in the funeral services and the pastoral care for the family, the congregation, the community and the community at camp. In that tragic and trying shared experience he and I truly became pastors for one another. We became Anam Cara. Since then we have shared experiences, travels, much laughter, various ups and downs, etc... we have and continue to be faithfully there for one another.

I am incredibly blessed in the relationships I have with my two sons, with my students, and with friends and colleagues throughout the church and the communities in which I have lived. Yet the Anam Cara that I have been blessed with are those who will walk right through the walls of time, space, ego and other barriers that I (like any person) will put up to try to cover and protect my frightened and vulnerable self. These soul friends know me, they know my story, they know my faults, they know my sins, they know my gifts, and they know my dreams. I have nothing that I have to hide from them and they have nothing left to hide from me. I thank God that I have these Anam Cara. I am deeply blessed.

Jesus knew that his disciples would need their own Anam Cara. He would be such while he was with them but they would also need to be so for one another. For their calling was not to be an easy journey - faithful life never is. Remember that during one phase of their training he sent them out two by two. On their long walks through the mountains and valleys, towns and villages of Palestine each had to learn to completely trust the other and to be fully open themselves to each other. They learned I think, what I have begun to understand, that it is only through experiencing Anam Cara relationships with others that we can fully enter into such a relationship, an Anam Cara relationship with God. This, I think, is among the most important lessons that Jesus wanted his disciples to learn and what I feel God hopes we too might also discover and learn. Therefore, if you have not already done so, take the risk, take the journey, be fully vulnerable with someone, make it mutual and find your Anam Cara. I know, easier said than done.

Family becoming friends

Friends are critically important. During this time in your life it is developmentally appropriate that you invest a great deal of your time and energy in establishing and strengthening friendships. (Perhaps a few who might become your Anam Cara – okay I'll stop.) According to various developmental theorists, this is among the key tasks of early and late adolescence. We establish an identity of self through social interactions with friends. It is our task to differentiate from our parents and to establish this identity of self.

Most of you are probably well on your way along this path of differentiation and identity establishment. But what about your family of origin, what about home?

During Jesus' ministry and instructional journeys with the disciples the canonical gospels indicate an on again/off again relationship with families of origin. Even Jesus it seems didn't know quite how to deal consistently with his mother and brothers. In the story of the Wedding of Cana there is this encounter between Jesus and his mom:

> *On the third day a wedding took place at Cana in Galilee. Jesus' mother was there, and Jesus and his disciples had also been invited to the wedding. When the wine was gone, Jesus' mother said to him, "They have no more wine."*
>
> *"Dear woman, why do you involve me?" Jesus replied, "My time has not yet come."*
>
> *His mother said to the servants, "Do whatever he tells you."* (John 2:1-5 NIV)

Here Mary seems to volunteer Jesus for something that he is not quite sure he wants to be involved in quite yet.

Has that ever happened to you? (No of course not...)

Then there is this passage from the Gospel of Matthew Chapter 12: 46-50 that I referenced earlier:

> *While Jesus was still talking to the crowd, his mother and brothers stood outside, wanting to speak to him. Someone told him, "Your mother and brothers are standing outside, wanting to speak to you." He replied to him, "Who is my mother, and who are my brothers?" Pointing to his disciples, he said, "Here are my mother and my brothers. For whoever does the will of my Father in heaven is my brother and sister and mother."(NIV)*

Admittedly, according to tradition, Jesus was now in his thirties and we assume had gone through the developmental process of differentiation and self-identification. We don't really know what the family of origin dynamic was between Jesus and his family at this point, but it seems that Jesus was seeking to expand the definition of "family". There is this series of encounters in the Gospel of Luke Chapter 9: 57-62:

As they were walking along the road, a man said to him, "I will follow you wherever you go." Jesus replied, "Foxes have holes and birds of the air have nests, but the Son of Man has no place to lay his head."

He said to another man, "Follow me." But the man replied, "Lord, first let me go and bury my father." Jesus said to him, "Let the dead bury their own dead, but you go and proclaim the kingdom of God."

Still another said, "I will follow you, Lord; but first let me go back and say good-by to my family." Jesus replied, "No one who puts his hand to the plow and looks back is fit for service in the kingdom of God."

Does it really surprise anyone that the relationship between these disciples, some of whom we assume were young adults, and their families were complicated? After all, they had gone off script to follow Jesus and to challenge the powers that be. In first century in Palestine there was a clear and absolute script to follow. You did what your family expected you to do, period, end of discussion. Now there was this Rabbi, calling all sorts of people to leave home, to follow him, and then saying, *"let the dead bury their own dead".* Not the sort of thing that encourages easy family relationships.

Try that sometime when your parents ask you what you are doing and who you are spending time with, "Does it really matter? Let the dead bury their own dead". The next thing you know, you'll get a call from someone asking you about your cult involvement.

This stuff screams of broken relationships with families of origin. Yet then there is the passage from Acts 1:14:

59

"They all joined together constantly in prayer, along with the women and Mary the mother of Jesus, and with his brothers."

Many biblical scholars seem to find that this passage in Acts indicates a moment of reconciliation between the disciples who were Jesus' chosen family and Mary and his brothers, who were Jesus' family of origin.

For the purposes of our explorations, these passages indicate the developmental struggle of reconciling one's relationships with friends who have become family and family becoming friends. You will need both your friends and your family as you continue to encounter transition periods and change factors throughout your life. Yet unless you begin or continue to "make the break" and to re-configure and re-define your relationship with your family of origin, you may not have a critical resource for your discernment process.

As I have written earlier, each semester I usually teach a first year seminar course. Especially in the fall, early in the semester I offer some advice, "Don't Go Home." (Sorry parents.) "Don't go home unless you absolutely have to do so". This is easy on football weekends, but I tell them to stay even when there are away games. I advise them that they need to stay in Boone because they need to meet people, they need to figure out what there is to do when it seems there is nothing to do, they need to go out and walk around, drive or walk around, get lost and then find their way back to a place they recognize. It is important for them to establish themselves where they are now in their new place. Some take my advice, but I think most go home anyway.

Then around Thanksgiving after most have fairly well settled in to college life, I begin to warn these first-year-folk that Thomas Wolfe was right, "you can't go home again". Then I explain what I think he meant. Even in a few short months they have changed, they have become different persons, so the person who goes "home" in November is not the same person who left home in August. If they are the same person, then those of us who teach and work with them are doing a lousy job. Following this little sermonette, I give them an assignment of one kind or another that helps them reflect on how they have changed and how their perception of home has changed.

You have now come through several years of such changes. Take a few moments and reflect on home:

- Where do you feel most at "home", in the home you left as a fresh-person or at college?
- How has your relationship with your family of origin changed in the past few years?
- Do you and your parents negotiate "the rules" when your go home or are you able to have the same freedom of coming and going that you know at college?
- How have you changed? Does going home seem to highlight some of these changes?

If you haven't done so before now, try this the next time you go home. Go visit your elementary school. Take a walk through the halls, visit a few of your teachers, step into a classroom, sit in a desk, or better yet go into one of the bathrooms in the area of the school for the youngest ages. It will become very obvious to you in a very short time that you have grown and changed a great deal since you were a student in that place. Not only have you grown physically, but of course you have grown intellectually, emotionally, socially, and hopefully spiritually. By returning to your elementary school you can very easily measure how you have grown both literally and figuratively.

Going back home can be helpful in much the same way. Noting how you have changed, and in effect measuring your growth, can help you become more attuned to the reality that change and growth are normal and necessary facts of life. You can no more return home the same person as you can return and be a student at your elementary school. You don't fit there anymore. It may be good to visit, but you now belong somewhere else.

Change and growth are easy to see in regards to physical places such as your elementary school, your room at home. Perhaps you even have a door frame on which your parents marked how you have grown physically. Throughout your school experiences there have been instruments to test and measure your intellectual growth. Yet it is more difficult to measure emotional, social, and spiritual growth. This is where your long term relationships, especially the relationships with your family such as your parents and your siblings can be very helpful. Your relationships and conversations with family, if pursued constructively, can be the reflective mirrors and/or reflective guides wherein you can get feedback on how you have grown emotionally, socially, and even spiritually. Consciously and/or sub-consciously they are aware that you have changed, because you have a different presence, a *different gravity* so to speak. You need them to tell you what they notice that is different.

Here is what I mean by gravity. I travel away from home fairly regularly in my ministry position. I lead mission trips, retreats, conferences, and I love to travel for pleasure and adventure. Even though Karen and I have a healthy marriage and she is my Anam Cara, we have learned that upon my return home from traveling of more than a day or two, we have to be aware of this thing we have come to call "re-entry". You won't remember, but back in the early days of the space program upon return to earth the astronauts would be required to spend a few days in isolation, re-adjusting to earth's gravity and adjusting to the atmosphere, as well as getting fully checked out and debriefed medically, emotionally, etc... . My re-entry, my return home is in some ways like this. Karen and I need time to sync up with one another and to adjust to one another's gravity, atmosphere and presence.

I don't know if you have experienced something like "re-entry" when you came home from college. Perhaps you have noticed that after the initial, "we're so glad you are home" that you find that you and your siblings and/or parents end up literally or more often figuratively bumping in to one another. It may have even resulted in some conflict. This is the re-entry or the syncing gravity of which I am referring. You all are just adjusting to the different gravity in the home, the changed atmosphere that is present because (and I don't mean this as negatively as it might sound), "because you came home and now everything is different!"

Human beings are like planets in this way. We become accustomed to our orbits and when another "heavenly body" enters the system, it affects our gravity and we must make adjustments. Like any change, it can be difficult.

Once you have adjusted to one another but perhaps before everything returns to normal (more liminal space, take note), I encourage you to have a conversation with one or both of your parents or perhaps a sibling if you have one still at home. Talk with them about you and ask them if they have noticed any changes and/or growth? How are you different now than when you left for school as a fresh-person? If they don't have much to say, then jump on in there and tell them what you notice about them. Tell them what you notice about yourself and ask them if they can see it? Tell them about what you are doing, your studies, your relationships, and your new interests. Talk with them about your dreams and visions and your new thoughts and ideas. In other words, take the time or make the time to have one of "those" conversations. You know, one of those conversations where your family can get to know you for who you are becoming. You know, one of those vulnerable, lay-it-out on the table, honest and real conversations with your family members (What? NO! Who? Not Me!) Nearly every time you go home, I suggest that you need to make sure that your family gets to know you once again, because each and every time you come home, unless it is way too regularly, you are in effect a different person. If for some reason you can't get this accomplished with a parent, then find a neighbor, a friend, a pastor. Find someone.

How does this apply for persons who have not moved away from home for college? It can happen when after days and days of routine when the family is orbiting in ordinary gravity, you take the step of calling a family meeting so you can talk with everyone. That is when you help everyone including yourself pay some attention to what has changed, how you have changed, etc... I guarantee that if you ask for a family meeting, the regular gravity of the family orbits will be shifted.

As I wrote earlier, among the developmental tasks necessary for becoming an adult is establishing self-identity and differentiation. Just as visiting the elementary school provides blatant proof that you have grown and changed. In the same way you coming home and having intentional conversation can help your family and help you see how you are growing and changing socially, emotionally and even spiritually. It may be difficult for your parents to adjust to you being an adult child never the less this is the task at hand for everyone. Your family will quickly adapt to your physical presence, your gravity, and you to theirs. However, you want to help them adapt to the other changes as well. You want to help them know you for who you are now, a young adult, and you should want to have a different relationship with them than the one you had with them while you were in high school. The healthiest way and most constructive way for this to happen are through conversation, through talking with one another. (I know it sounds crazy! What am I saying?)

Once you take the step and help this happen, once you begin to talk and communicate with folks at home in an open and healthy way, home can become a very rich resource for your discernment process. (Ah hah! You knew we would be coming back to this!)

Now that you have begun to establish your self-identity and differentiation, home and the folks who are there can be excellent reflective guides for you along your journey. After all, they have known you and traveled with you in one way or another for your whole life. They can be your consistent mirror. If you have a relatively healthy relationship (and I know way too many of these relationships are not healthy), your parents, your siblings, your grandparents, and others at home can provide love and support like few others. Even if the relationship are not so healthy, working on and perhaps healing or at least learning the realities of the relationships can be helpful and necessary steps in your discernment.

I've heard it said that families are a great laboratory for life. Families are the people with whom God gives us to experiment, to test, to try, to fail and occasionally succeed. Through this experimentation we learn about living with other people and perhaps even learn how to do it successfully. It is within the context of family where we come to understand basic tools of life like sharing, confrontation, and forgiveness.

Through college and following, your relationship with your parents, siblings and others in your family will be changing significantly, yet the experimental and experiential laboratory that is family can and will continue to a place of great learning for you.

These experiments and conversations with the folks back home can and should be very critical parts of your discernment. Remember the futuring scenarios diagram from Chapter 1? It is a critical element of this methodology to establish current trend or trajectory. Home is part of how this happens. Home is critical to your discernment process. By going home you have the opportunity to reflect upon your growth with those who know you from early on and in effect you have a chance like no other to measure your growth in a literal and/or figurative sense. You can test your theories about yourself and have these theories affirmed or adjusted. Where have you been? Where are you going really? Home can be an anchor point, a starting point for this line which you can work with as the line of your trajectory thus far. Your line begins here in the family in which you were raised. There have been shifts, change factors, and adjustments and your line has passed through these changes bending up, down or remaining level. You are on a trajectory, but which line is yours? Those who know you best can help you identify your trend line.

Which line is your trajectory/trend line? As you approach the change factor of graduation?

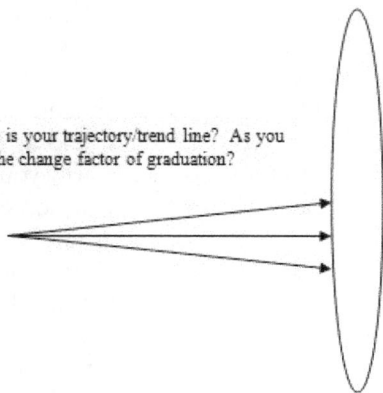

Putting this all into question form, *how can you begin to know where you are heading if you haven't yet discerned where you have been?* This is why heading for home can be so helpful. Home is your history. Some people's history is not so pretty. However, it is from here you can measure how far you have come and in what direction you have traveled. I was at point A, now I am at point B. Connect the points and you have your line, though it may be a crooked one. Once your specific trajectory is discerned, you can then begin to look towards the future, past the change factor of graduation. Where would you like to go? How would you like to get there? The script which is now blank simply implies improvise and adapt.

A brief rant on moving home

Sometimes it is necessary to go home and stay there for a while. In the economic realities of the latter twentieth and early twenty first centuries, this has become more and more common. Young adults sometimes find that they need such a safety net. After all, just as the disciples had the sanctuary of the upstairs room where the basics were covered, as I wrote earlier, you may need to return home during your discernment as a means of covering the basics. This is fine. No worries.

However, it was never the intention for the disciples to stay for very long there in the upstairs room. This was always to be a temporary sanctuary, a Third Place, but never home. Their lives were to be lived elsewhere. It is kind of like the mountaintop I spoke of in Chapter 2. Home, like a mountaintop, is a great place to gain perspective, to get your bearings, and as I have just said "home is your history". But it is not necessarily your future.

For many young people who move back home following college or a time away from home, they often fall back into old patterns. Remember the planet metaphor? After the heavenly bodies have re-adapted to one another it is very easy for them to fall into the familiar orbits of the past. Your family loves you (I assume) and you love them (again assumption.) Therefore everyone tries to avoid the inevitable conflict that is present, ignoring the fact that the gravity has changed and that these orbits really no longer fit the reality of the planetary system. Despite their best efforts, they are regularly bumping into one another and having conflicts which seem never to get resolved.

I hold the young adult responsible. *Yes, you.* If this happens to you and you find yourself long term temporarily moving back home, which you very well might, then you need to be responsible for and respectful of the fact that you have created a situation that has confused everyone's orbits. You are the cause of all this bumping into one another and the confusion of the system. Therefore it is your responsibility to make sure that some process of intentional re-entry takes place. The members of the system will need to have a sit-down down conversation about expectations, responsibilities, and respect. I also suggest documenting the expectations on both sides. It is wrong for you to expect to come back home and expect everything to adjust and adapt to you. As you may realize as you gain consciousness and awareness, you also will need to do a great deal of adjusting and adapting to this familiar yet unfamiliar planetary system.

My concern for you is that by moving home your trend line/trajectory will meet a stop sign or more concerning that it will actually reverse. Your family loves you (I assume), and they want to help you in what is often a difficult, confusing, and frightening adjustment to not having a script to follow. So, out of love, they will allow you to come back home and to some extent follow a part of the script that you know so well, that of child. The problem is you are no longer just a child; you are now an *adult* child. You have had and probably want to continue having a different orbit. Without you at home they have become used to a different orbit. CRASH!!!!

So once again, if this happens, take responsibility as an adult child to negotiate your orbits and your expectations. Give and get. Work out the details of the living arrangements including household chores, when you are coming home (or not coming home), occasional face time, etc.... Understand that this was probably not in your parent's or sibling's script for you and they are busy re-writing as well. If done well, this extended time at home can be a rich time of discernment and of developing a new adult child to adult parent relationship. This new relationship can become a mutually supportive and mutually challenging relationship that can enrich both you and your parents. But this does not happen, and will not happen, if you all are not intentional about making it happen.

Finally (sermon/rant coming to conclusion), in your negotiations and during regular check-ins you will want to use something like the futuring scenario methodology to project a best case/worst case scenario for your moving out and on.

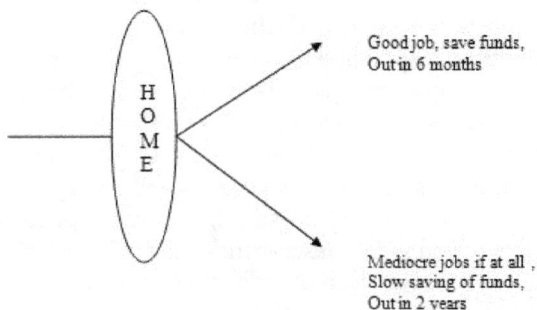

What choices can you make now that will help even this scenario trend towards your best case scenario? That is unless you really want to live in your parent's home for most of your twenties and basically live like a kid in high school? Have you seen the movie *Failure to Launch?* This isn't the life you are called to live. Remember what Jesus said about putting your hand to the plow... and about going back to bury the dead? I think he meant something like "living doesn't happen in reverse – keep moving forward".

What, Where, Who and then How

Let's review. You've come down into the valley following graduation and begun to do something – there is your *what*. You've realized that you are in an in between kind of time, space and place – there is your *where*. Now you've begun to gather with some others who are either "family", friends, or even really family – there is your *who*.

Having these are critical steps in beginning to write your own script on those blank pages you found on the other side of graduation. You now have some actions (little though it may be).

You have a location, which is pretty cool because the Third Place you have found will be a great place for just hanging out during parts of the story. You also have some characters beyond yourself, which is a good thing because a script needs dialogue. Monologue is booooooooring. *What, where, who* – good. In the next chapter we'll dig into *how.* There are some technical skills that you might need to pick up so you can navigate well along the way you may follow.

But Wait.

When?

Not yet.

Chapter 4
Wondering *How?*

Waiting Sucks

If you are like me, and I think most of us in the Western world are, we hate to wait. Very few things frustrate me as much as useless waiting, like waiting for a delayed flight or waiting in a traffic jam or waiting too long at a restaurant. I mean really! You plan your trip, you pack your bags, you arrive at the airport on time, you rush through check-in, wait "patiently" in the security line, and then arrive at the gate and then... and then... and then... you find that the flight is delayed and all you can do is wait. It is out of your control, you've done everything you can possibly think of and now all you can do is wait. Waiting sucks! That's all there is too it.

For many the post-college experience is very much a series of frustrating waits. First there is the job wait. You have done what is in your control, you have followed the script; followed a course of study, done some career counseling, completed at least one summer internship, graduated (maybe even with honors), and have put yourself out there on the job market. Now all you can do is wait. It is out of your control, and you hate it. What else can you do?

Then there is the relationship waiting. Waiting for the right relationship of the significant sort, the sustainable sort, the one the script said you are supposed to be finding sometime in the not-too-distant future. You know the one that so many of your old friends seem to have found already. You feel like you have done what you can. You've put yourself "out there" as much as you really care to do. You have let your friends know that they are welcome to introduce you to someone they might know but who also needs to be more than "such a nice girl or guy". You have even considered doing the internet thing, match.com, chemistry.com or one of the others, but you are not quite there

70

yet. So at this point you are just waiting and you are okay with that for now.

Since you are waiting on a job and a relationship, this kind of puts the whole getting settled and living your life thing in a waiting mode as well. Why would you commit to a community if you don't know where your job will be and if you have no idea who you might be living with? All of life, in one way or another, seems on hold. Your life is waiting for the pieces to fall into place. It isn't that you are really in a great hurry. You kind of like parts of your life right now, the freedom, no classes, and few commitments. In fact, if it weren't for the money thing, the covering the basics thing, this wouldn't be such a bad life. At times you find yourself saying "I could do this awhile." Yet at other times you feel the push, the expectations, that old script. You hear parents and others saying, in subtle if not so subtle ways, "get on with it, you have to start sometime and it might as well be now."

Then there is graduate school. Are you really considering going back to school for another degree? Didn't you just finish seventeen years of school? If you go back into academics it seems like you're just putting real life on hold for another two or three years, especially if you are still not sure about what you want to be doing in life anyway. You would have to take the GRE/MCAT/LCAT then figure out the programs and schools you are interested in and then wait. WAIT?

One of the things about waiting is that if you know to expect it then it really isn't too bad. It is the unexpected waiting that is usually so frustrating. For example, if you look ahead and know that flights at the airport are going to be delayed you can bring a good book and wait patiently. If you know that traffic is going to be slow and there will be some waiting, you can either map a different course or make sure you have a good book and/or music on the system. If you know the restaurant is usually slow then you plan to only go there with good friends, schedule the time, and order a good bottle of wine and some appetizers to enjoy while great conversation fills the wait. So it isn't the wait so much that is frustrating but rather the fact that you didn't know it was coming and you didn't have a chance to make the most of the wait.

If you are getting ready to graduate, if you are getting ready for a major life transition, *if you are traveling anywhere by airline*, chances are good that you are in for some waiting. *That last one is just helpful advice.* The other two are really what I want to dig into. Since you are more than likely in a hurry to get to the finish line take a moment and consider how you might make the most of your wait time. As I have written before the things you do now to learn how to transition and how to make the most of the wait will help you through such times that will surely come at other stages and transition points in your life.

Prayerful Waiting

In our now familiar passage from Acts 1, we learn that the disciples and the small reconciled community of Jesus' family and friends were there in the upstairs room waiting for what comes next. Jesus had given them the suggestion that there would be something and/or someone coming on whom they needed to wait. This someone or something was the Holy Spirit. Whatever that is? During this time of waiting Luke writes that the disciples were "*constantly devoting themselves in prayer*".

Over the centuries much has been written and spoken on the topic of prayer. Thousands of books, articles and blogs are available covering types of prayers, prayer practices, guides for prayers, collections of prayers of famous people, etc.... I encourage you, if interested, to dig into resources that help you with your own disciplines and practices of prayer. Certainly prayer is something that could fill a time of waiting; however it is not my purpose here to delve deeply into the topic and/or types of prayer. Others have covered this more than adequately. I am, however, intrigued by the statement "*constantly devoting themselves in prayer*".

If you are like me the image that first comes to mind when reading the statement, *constantly devoting themselves in prayer*, is of the disciples and their friends down on their knees 24/7, heads bowed, hands folded. For days and days, week after week, this whole group is praying and only taking turns to eat, sleep, and go to the bathroom. Otherwise pray, pray, pray, like the most devout monks. But then I remember who these folks really were. They were basically clueless and human just like you and me. They were real, which is why Jesus asked these to follow him. He asked these folks, rather than the hyper-religious types who were plentiful in that place and period of Jewish history.

Once I allow the disciples to step down from the pedestal, my image shifts. I hope yours does as well. Now we can imagine that during these days and nights following the Ascension and preceding Pentecost, the upstairs room was anything but quiet. Instead of silent prayer, I imagine fairly constant conversations. Throughout each day there was coming and going, preparations for meals, re-negotiations of arrangements with their host ("what do you mean you don't know when you are leaving?"). You know, all that regular daily life. Yet throughout this living, Luke was still right when he wrote this line here in Acts. For in spite of all this activity and conversation, they were indeed *constantly devoting themselves in prayer.* Prayer happens in lots of forms.

More often than not when we, who are awash in western Christian culture (whether we like it or not), consider prayer or when we practice prayer ourselves it is in time set-apart and separate from our daily lives. We come by this honestly. For this is the tradition we inherit. Through the centuries of religious interpretation and practice in western Roman Christianity, prayer is a practice that is separated dualistically, the sacred from the profane. Yet there are many other traditions of prayer from which to draw. Among them is the Celtic Christian spiritual traditions still hanging on and being recovered. In this tradition prayer was not a separate practice but rather one that was included in even the most mundane and profane moments of daily life. Among the prayers collected by Alexander Carmichael during the late nineteenth century on the Islands of the Outer Hebrides in Scotland, which he compiled in a work known as the <u>Carmina Gadelica</u> or *Songs of the Gaels*, were prayers for a variety of common daily activities. This prayer is a blessing sung during the milking of cows:

> *Columba will give to her progeny,*
> *Coivi the propitious, will give to her grass,*
> *My speckled heifer will give me her milk,*
> *And her female calf before her.*
> *Ho my heifer! heifer! heifer!*
> *Ho my heifer! kindly, calm,*

My heifer gentle, gentle, beloved,
Thou art the love of thy mother.
Seest yonder thriving bramble bush
And the other bush glossy with brambles,
Such like is my fox-coloured heifer,
And her female calf before her.
Ho my heifer! -
The calm Bride of the white combs
Will give to my loved heifer the lustre of the swan,
While the loving Mary, of the combs of honey,
Will give to her the mottle of the heather hen.
Ho my heifer! -

In this tradition, prayers of labor, prayers for sleeping, prayers for eating, prayers for all of life's daily activities were common. There were certainly prayers to fill every moment of the day, even times of waiting. Conversations with God were constant. Because God is constantly present. Rather than being separated into sacred and profane spaces, heaven and earth are understood as both being the realm of God. Therefore prayer was not a practice only for sacred space and sacred times, but rather for all times, all spaces, and all practices. Prayer, like breathing in and breathing out, could become "constant".

In his wonderful introduction to Celtic Christian Spirituality *Listening for the Heartbeat of God*, J. Phillip Newell writes concerning the prayers/songs collected by Carmichael:

> *"The emphasis in these prayers on the goodness of the earth and the belief that God's dwelling-place is deep within creation is a further reflection and development of the interweaving of the spiritual and the material exemplified by the art of the old Celtic Church, where the patterns of heaven and earth intertwine and overlap. So to look to God is not to look away from life but to look more deeply into it. Together with this emphasis on the presence of God at the heart of creation, of God being the heartbeat of life, there is also a sense of the closeness, not only of God but of the whole host of heaven, enfolding the earth and its people with love."*

The disciples and the early followers knew God in their midst, knew this presence intimately in the person of Jesus. With Jesus they had lived each moment of life profane, sacred and profound. They had lived each moment not as an experience of separateness but rather as an experience of deep incarnation, *intimate human and divine present-ness*. It is only later that the western church guided by a deep philosophical leaning towards platonic dualism (you knew I would come back to it) began to isolate and separate the sacred (Holy) from the profane (common). Therefore I think we need to re-imagine the upstairs room during those first days and months and years. When we hear or read the words *"constantly devoting themselves to prayer"*, instead of 24/7 down on one's knees in silence, we can now imagine deep, caring, imaginative, insightful conversations held within the comings and goings of everyday life. Through their conversations and interactions with one another and with the world about them the disciples simultaneously included and invoked and involved God in the midst of their conversations.

Though they were waiting for what comes next, the Holy Spirit, it wasn't empty waiting. The disciples filled their time with intentional and prayerful conversations, with intentional and prayerful activities, with intentional and prayerful time together as community. In our predominantly western way of viewing the world (yes dualistic) there is purposeful time and there is wasted time. Waiting is more often than not understood to be wasted time. Yet, in relationship with God, with God's creation and with one another, there is no such thing as wasted time. There is simply time. There is the time we have and we are to make the most of the time we have.

Hold on. Check that. When our puritan influenced ears hear the statement *making the most*, we feel the need to be doing something obviously constructive and obviously purposeful. Clear out your ears and hear that all time is God's time even the times we are waiting and doing "nothing".

Let's go back to the airport. (Do we have to? Yes, just for a brief personal example.) When I allow myself to let go of my need to be in control and schedule every moment of my day with some sort of "productivity", I usually find rest and/or re-creativity while waiting. As I suggested, if I know it is coming, waiting can be a great time. I'll read and/or write or better yet I'll have a conversation with someone that I've never met. I'll explore the airport and find something new or I'll simply close my eyes and listen to the life around me.

Making the Most of Times Like These

This brings me to a deeper discussion of Sabbath time. You are probably too young but I remember Sundays like they used to be. Oh yes we still have Sunday as a day of the week on the calendar, but in our 24/7 culture of nearly constant production and consumption, most of us don't really have anything like Sundays or Sabbath. Remember that Sabbath is one of God's big ten from Exodus 20 *"remember the Sabbath and keep it Holy"* or in the recap of the big ten from Deuteronomy 5 *"remember the Sabbath."* Somewhere along the way we lost or gave away our Sundays in exchange for convenience. Sure, we might go to worship, but then often the day is like every other day, filled with activities, comings and goings, producing and consuming. It was becoming less common even when I was young, having Sundays as a day of rest. Such days were slipping away. But I do remember vestiges of such days, such Sundays, at least at a very young age in Virginia and then in Florida. Since the stores were closed you couldn't go shopping and most people didn't have to go to work. You couldn't work for the most part because there weren't computers and e-mail and cell phones. The only calls you made were to family and friends and you had to know them pretty well because you didn't want to disturb their Sunday. Families and friends would often gather for Sunday dinner which was often a pot-luck, a pot-roast, or a picnic. Even my Mom and Dad, who tended to work on Sundays because we had groups at camp until after lunch, would often find time for a Sunday afternoon nap. The work at camp could wait until Monday. Now it seems nothing much can wait, even for Sunday, even for Sabbath.

(But I wax nostalgic. Sorry.) I'm not the only one. Here is another passage from Lauren Winner's book *Mudhouse Sabbath:*

"... there is something in the Jewish Sabbath that is absent from most Christian Sundays: a true cessation from the rhythms of work and world, a time wholly set apart, and, perhaps above all, a sense that the point of Shabbat, the orientation of Shabbat, is toward God."

Among the things that we have lost in giving up our Sundays and/or Sabbaths are the lessons of stillness, the lessons of waiting, the lessons of patience, and the lessons of Sabbath time. Among the curses of contemporary western culture is the curse of instant gratification. We just can't wait to get and to have what we want. We know what we want and we want it now! The amazing, yet sad thing is most of us can usually "get it now 24/7/365". Therefore we have little opportunity to learn some of the basic lessons of life, such as *it isn't about you. Life does not revolve around you and your needs and your desires and your appetites.* We don't learn these lessons and therefore when we don't get what we want, NOW, like a job and a life and a partner right when we should, when it is expected, right when it is supposed to come in the script, we become frustrated and impatient with ourselves and with others. Someone is to blame and among all the others at fault, some of it must be God's fault as well.

Among all the other lessons that might be learned in the unscripted time following graduation, this is a great time to learn once more or for the first time if you haven't already, *that it isn't all about you. You are not the center of the Universe despite what your mom or your dad told you when you were little (last year). So sit down, be still, and wait your turn you spoiled brat!* (Of course that is all said with love.)

Times of waiting like Sabbath observance/remembrance can and should be such times of learning and re-learning, reflection and observation, stillness and being. Becoming acquainted or re-acquainted with such time is a gift and can be received as such. A young woman who graduated several years ago came into my office recently. She is a very gifted, bright, talented young woman. She spent a year in an Episcopal sponsored internship in Washington D.C. serving a variety of service and mission roles. At the time of our conversation, she had completed her year and was back in the area. She had not yet lined up plans for what comes next. When she came to see me of course I asked her, "What are you going to

77

be doing?" She basically said, "For a while, I'm just going to be". Her plan, at least for that time, was to revel in the grace of being, to take time to reflect on her year of service in mission, and to wait patiently and prayerfully to discern what comes next. Good for her.

In river terms (metaphor warning!) she is taking some time to eddy out and to look both back towards the river she has traveled and ahead towards the river to come. The eddy is a Sabbath moment, a grace moment, a time offered to rest and re-orient before moving back into the flowing stream.

In the coming months and perhaps years following graduation you may find yourself in such a time of waiting, in just such a river eddy. Though it is certainly easier said than done, rather than becoming frustrated and impatient with waiting, you may find grace in simply being and resting there in the still water. You may discover a sense of Sabbath as time and life oriented towards God. You may prayerfully take the time and have the conversations through which you might discern God's desires for you and calling to you for the next phase of your life. The river will be there; it isn't going anywhere. So I encourage you to "make the most of your time" and take the intentional and purposeful time that you need.

Learning from Rivers

If you have never canoed or rafted on a river, you may be wondering about my references to eddys and to rivers. Rivers are among my favorite metaphors for life and I am certainly not alone in this. I think it has to do with the fact that from a very young age I have lived on or near one river or another. At Cedarkirk, the camp where I was raised in Florida, I paddled an inner-tube or canoe down the Alafia River at least once a week on average from the time that I was eleven until I was twenty. I came to know that river intimately and in time I learned to read the changing currents so I could paddle various courses depending on the trip I wanted to take. If I wanted an adventurous ride, I would follow one course, if I wanted a smooth ride I could choose another. The course I traveled along the river was basically the same, a 12-mile stretch from Alderman's Ford down to Lithia Springs, but each trip along this course was unique each of the hundreds of times I paddled.

There are so many ways that human lives are like rivers, so authors, poets, artists, preachers and others have filled volumes with examples. Jesus and his disciples knew the Jordan River and the lessons it offers as it begins coursing down the slopes of Mt. Hermon high above sea level, then it forms flowing rapids north of Galilee, then becomes the freshwater lake known in scripture as the Sea of Galilee, then it continues along a tranquil course until it ends in the salty Dead Sea in desert climes 1300 feet below sea level (all of this in only 158 miles!)

As in life, a river's journey is segmented into sections of slow and rapid waters. Through the slow segments, a paddler pretty much wants to find the main channel where the waters are moving at a steady pace. Or if one chooses, you can simply float along, letting the current do all the work. However, when a paddler encounters rapids, especially bigger rapids filled with boulders and large standing waves known as whitewater, it is important for the paddler to take some time to stop and read the river, or more accurately to take the time to read the rapids. When choosing your course through the rapids it is important to consider a variety of factors including those within your control:

- ☐ Your level of experience in paddling through whitewater. Have you done this before?
- ☐ Your boat. Is it designed for whitewater or are you in a flat-water canoe?
- ☐ Your companions. Who is along for the ride and what are their choices?
- ☐ Your other equipment including your flotation device. If you fall out will you float or possibly sink?

It is also important to consider the variety of factors that are basically out of your control:

- ☐ The river's power on a particular day. Is there more or less volume of water due to rainfall or dam release?
- ☐ The rocks you can see and the rocks you can't see. It is always the ones you can't see that can cause the problems.

79

◻   Other canoes, kayaks or rafts. Someone else may be where you would like to go.

Through the years of running rapids a standard scale and description has been developed as follows. This may serve as a guide for which course to choose: (International Whitewater Scale according to Wikipedia)

Class I: Easy. Waves small; passages clear; no serious obstacles.

Class II: Medium. Rapids of moderate difficulty with passages clear. Requires experience plus suitable outfit and boat.

Class III: Difficult. Waves numerous, high, irregular; rocks; eddies; rapids with passages clear though narrow; requiring expertise in maneuvering; scouting usually needed. Requires good operator and boat.

Class IV: Very difficult. Long rapids; waves high, irregular; dangerous rocks; boiling eddies; best passages difficult to scout; scouting mandatory first time; powerful and precise maneuvering required. Demands expert boatman and excellent boat and good quality equipment.

Class V: Extremely difficult. Exceedingly difficult, long and violent rapids, following each other almost without interruption; riverbed extremely obstructed; big drops; violent current; very steep gradient; close study essential but often difficult. Requires best person, boat, and outfit suited to the situation. All possible precautions must be taken.

Class VI (or U) Unrunnable.

Once you take the time to consider these and other factors that are within or without of your control it is time to commit to a specific course through the rapids. Of course one option is always to portage around the rapids, meaning to carry your boat along the shore downriver until there is calm water once again. But if you choose to go on through here is what you will likely experience.

80

Before you there will be several channels which show themselves with what paddlers call tongues, these are V shaped currents that flow into the rapids. Beyond the tongues will be waves and rocks of various sizes and shapes. The waves are formed by rocks below the surface of the water which force the water up or to one side or another. Your canoe/kayak/raft will be forced to flow with the current which is the flow over, around, or even under the rocks. (The latter is what you really want to avoid.) Yet by paddling and steering you can influence your ride through the rapids either letting it ride, bouncing the rocks, riding the waves, or even eddying out to take another look.

Here is a description of a Class V Rapid known as *Insignificant* along the Upper Gauley River in West Virginia

"During the fall release, it is a big, long and squirrelly Class V+ rapid. The entrance is a tight and technical rock-garden with several small ledges and holes that can easily bump or spin the raft off-course. There is very little time to regain control before the second drop – a meaty ledge with a nasty pour-over that divides the river. Quick decision-making is required to make the move left or right of this juicy hole. Past the ledge the river narrows, gaining speed and driving all the water toward the right shore and into Slide Rock, a giant, house-sized boulder that slants into the river. As the water hits this rock, it explodes back into the main current creating a roller-coaster wave-train and holes that make for a good soaking. Don't worry if at the bottom of the run you have to shake your head and wonder what just happened, many guides have done the exact same thing!" (ACE Adventure Resort, Oak Hill, WV, brochure Fall 2009 Gauley Season Promotion)

I've had the experience of canoeing and rafting through some fairly major rapids on a variety of rivers including the Gauley, the New, the French Broad, the Ocoee, the Snake, the Nantahala, and the Shubenacadie. Before each large rapid I feel somewhat wary and following each ride I feel very alive. Having passed through the rough waters there is often a feeling of "what just happened". Some people talk of conquering rivers. I say they haven't paddled through enough whitewater. No one can conquer or control a river, though many have tried. Rivers are like life, we're subject to the current for the most part and simply trying our best to discern the course that is best for us.

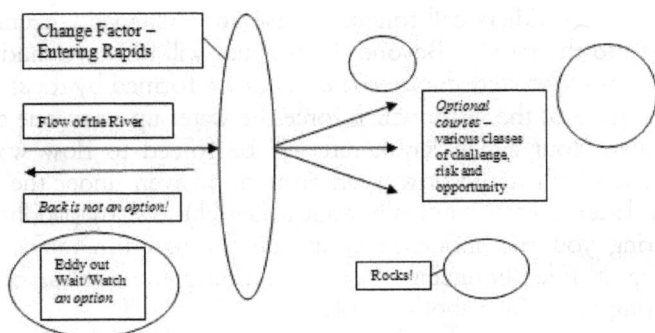

Change Factor – Entering Rapids

Flow of the River

Back is not an option!

Eddy out Wait/Watch *an option*

Optional courses – various classes of challenge, risk and opportunity

Rocks!

Prayerful Discernment

So now we've come back around to Discernment. In Chapter 2, I wrote about how through reflection on the choices and decisions made during transitional moments in our lives we can perhaps discern how this has impacted the course we have traveled thus far on our journey. At each point we either consciously or unconsciously made choices or decisions that either changed our course (for better or worse) or kept us on pretty much the same course. I encouraged this exercise of reflection as a way of understanding how each of us, through free will, might clearly influence the course of our life's journey. In our river metaphor, we have the choice of certain paddle strokes and steering maneuvers as we move down river. But for the most part our course is determined by the river's current. We also have the choice of opting out of certain experiences for now, Class III, IV, V rapids and waiting until we are better equipped to handle them. The only option we don't have in life is going backwards. Life is never lived in reverse though many try. Going back, paddling upstream, especially in rapids is just too much work to keep at for long. All the effort simply keeps you in place and you find yourself basically at a stand-still.

Human beings also don't have a whole lot of choice about the specific river we find ourselves on. I could be wrong, but it has been my experience that every person does not have unlimited and total freedom to choose the way he/she lives her/his life.

82

There are pre-determined variables based on family, culture, country and other factors into which individuals are born. However, within these variables and occasionally outside of those parameters, each person has choices to make (more on this in a moment). Suffice it to say that for those born into middle to upper-middle class families in late twentieth/early twenty-first century America and who have had the opportunity to attend college or university, you have had very broad parameters for your choice and decisions.* The river of your life is relatively wide and smooth. It is a river filled with channels of varying depths and types of currents. There may be a few rapids to ride through, but for the most part you know these have been passed through before and for the most part you can purchase all the right equipment at your local outfitter. The rivers are very different in many other parts of the world and especially for those without the resources to safely navigate the rapids or waterfalls of life. Try floating through a class V rapid without a raft, a helmet, a paddle, or a life preserver. Without the resources of our contemporary western culture even the same river can be a very different experience.

Yet this luxury of resources begets a conundrum of choices. I assume because most of you who are reading this book have had access to so many resources, because you have so many rich experiences, because you have such a large safety net, you often suffer from what I'll call option overload. Basically we find ourselves on a river that resembles the Amazon at high water.

Even 500 miles from the mouth of the river, at high water the Amazon can be 90 miles wide and filled with islands and channels and options. Which channel should you choose in order to stay on the course you wish to travel? When there are 90 miles of river to choose from the choices can be overwhelming and you can quickly become disoriented and even lost.

*I realize that there are many young adults who have not had these experiences and who do not have the access to the overwhelming resources and options of which I write. My career has been working with and having experience with middle to upper-middle class students. It is to this group that this issue of *overwhelming options and perhaps much of the book is primarily relevant. If this is not your experience then you are blessed because this is not your struggle.*

Here is another story that might clarify my meaning. When I was a teenager at Cedarkirk in Florida, the camp hosted Christmas International House. This program provided a home for students from abroad studying at colleges and universities throughout the United States. Since we were in Florida, near Disney World, Busch Gardens, and beaches, Cedarkirk was a very popular site for this program. One night during their two week stay at the camp we would hold an International Dinner where individuals or groups from various countries or cultures would prepare dishes from their homes. I loved this dinner and would help out by taking various students into town to buy the ingredients or the closest thing we could find. I remember taking a graduate student from Ghana into town to procure what was needed for his dish. When we came to the grocery store and we walked down isle after isle looking for this or that ingredient, he said to me, "Tommy, how do you do this every day? There are just too many choices, too many options. It makes my brain hurt."

This event with my West African friend took place in the 1970s. Since then our options in the West have grown exponentially. Our brains must hurt! It is not uncommon for me to meet with students whose primary problem seems to be that they have too many options to consider. Back in the days when the "script" still mattered, one was at least limited to some extent by whether you were male or female, or by whom your parents were and what your father did for a living, or by what region of the country you planned to live and work. Back then it seemed to matter more what major you chose and what career track you set. It mattered because the script had at least some pages following graduation that were determined by those choices or circumstances. However, as I've written before, those days are past and the script is mostly blank beyond graduation and/or filled with nearly unbounded options. This is why I suggest prayer.

In such moments, in such periods of discernment, it is helpful to pray. It is helpful because it is important to remember

84

that you cannot control the river after all. It is important to pray because, like Sabbath, it orients us towards God and reminds us once again that the universe does not revolve around us. It reminds us that we are simply riding upon the surface of the waters and that there are depths and life and levels of life within the currents of the river that we cannot easily comprehend. Prayer, done well, reminds us that we are but creatures. We are creatures created, loved, and for some reason loved and claimed by God. Prayer is and should be a practice of humility and humbleness. In all of our prayerful conversations, in all of our prayerful waiting, in all of our prayerful discernment, one of the realizations should be; *it really doesn't matter after all. I really don't matter after all.*

Then in the same breath, in the same thought, in the same prayer comes the realization that *it does matter! I do matter in as much as I flow with rather than fight the waters of life. I am one with the water and with all of life and therefore I matter.*

If you go on a rafting trip on a big whitewater river you will be given one very important set of instructions. This is; if you fall out of the raft and find yourself floating away from the raft through the rapids, Do Not Try To Stand Up. *Put your feet up on the surface in front of you, face downstream and go with the flow.*

The danger in standing up in rapids lies in the rocks below the surface. It is more than possible that if you try walking or standing on your own, stupidly fighting the river, then you will get your foot lodged in between rocks and you will be trapped, pushed under the water by the current, and possibly drown.

Here is another great metaphor from the river. Western individualism teaches us that we are responsible for ourselves alone and that we must learn to fight and scrap and bend and break the world to meet our needs. We are to pull ourselves up by our bootstraps and save ourselves. In other words, we are taught to stand up in the river and fight our way to the closest shore, "to hell with the rafts and the rapids." Yet the lesson of the river and rapids is, don't fight it. If you get in the right position, go with the flow, then watch and wait for the raft and for your mates to pull you back in. I think this is comparable to what the prophet Michah speaks when he says "Seek Justice, Love Kindness, and Walk Humbly with God." It is about knowing that the river is

85

greater than you and there is a proper orientation when you are in the midst of the wild waters, which is *humbleness.* Then there is waiting for your mates to pull you back in the raft, which is *loving kindness.* Then there is the opportunity to do the same for others who have fallen out of their rafts or are simply riding without flotation through the rapids, which is *seeking justice.*

All of this is to say that it doesn't really matter which path you choose, even when you have hundreds of options. The river is going to end up in the same place. The choice is much more about *how* rather than *what.* The decisions and discernment are about orientation rather than precise course and direction. Remember the David Wilcox song and story? God's desire is not to trip you up and watch you fall. You are designed by God to float on the waters. Therefore if you take the time to look ahead and to discern what rapids are passable with the resources and experience you and your raft mates bring to the task. Then wisely decide what Class IV, V, or V+ rapids you might want to save for later in your life's journey after you have more resources and experience. Finally, you simply portage your way around those impassable Class VI waterfalls. If you take the time to prayerfully wait, have prayerful conversations, and prayerfully discern, then you know what? You are going to have a great ride down the river of life. It won't always be a smooth ride, but it will be an experience because you have focused more on *how* you are doing life rather than *what* you are doing in life.

So once again, *how are you doing?*

The Action of Prayerful Waiting

Despite what it may have seemed and how we interpret what we read, the disciples were doing a great deal. They were prayerfully waiting while living their lives. They were finding their way in the flow of life. Because prayer was an integral part of their days, they could trust the flow and not fight it. Though it seemed like they were not doing much of anything, they were actually beginning, perhaps for the first time, to do exactly what Jesus had

86

requested. In prayerfully waiting while living, their lives were becoming a witness in Jerusalem. They were discovering their *how.*

So now we have a *how* to go along with our *what, where* and *who.* Our script is finding a starting point (just after graduation), a location (down in the valleys), a cast of characters (you, your "family", and your family), and now with *how* we can begin to navigate a story line (moving forward). We also know that there will be adventure in the rapids, drama in the struggles, comedy in the errors made and lessons to be learned.

Now you are beginning to have something to work with! It is time to begin.

When?

Now!

Chapter 5
Wondering *When?*

Doing Nothing Really?

I will almost guarantee you that sometime in the next few years you are going to hear yourself saying, "I am not doing anything important." After nearly twenty years of being a full or even part-time student and somehow meeting all the expectations and requirements, you will come to a point where you feel like you are doing nothing or at least doing nothing of value. There are no papers to write, no assignments to finish, no books you have to read, and no classes to attend. If you have been lucky enough to find a job, it is probably not one that you feel is using you to your full potential. It is likely the jobs you will find following graduation and even in the first five years or so are more entry level position, something to get your foot in the door. Even if your new work is within your field of interest, you haven't begun at the level or position that you had hoped. You end up doing a lot of basic tasks, the grunt work, and often it feels like *you are doing nothing of value.*

Perhaps you expected this to a point. You probably were told by someone along the way, perhaps your parents, your professor, your friends, or even the person who hired you, "that you have to begin somewhere." Yet you ask yourself, "Does that somewhere have to be so meaningless and dull?" On top of this you perhaps come to realize that even a $25,000.00 starting salary really isn't much money. At least it is not as much as it first sounded. After paying rent, utilities, insurance, taxes, student loan payments, etc... you hardly have enough funds left for entertainment. (So much for your goin' clubin'.) So you find yourself working 45-50 hours each week (not including your commute in traffic) then coming back to your apartment and watching TV or a movie, or just getting on the internet. You look forward to the weekends and you try to plan and arrange something fun, but everything costs so much money! Not to mention the friends scenario from back in Chapter 2. Eventually you and the friends you can find decide to get together, have dinner, and watch a movie (but isn't that what you did every other night this week?) Once again you wonder "am I doing anything, really?"

It is at this point perhaps that you begin to realize that you are in the midst of your very own "quarterlife crisis". In the book *Quarterlife Crisis* by Abby Wilner and Alexandra Robbins, the writers address the critical transitional struggles faced by many twenty-somethings in their transition from college to what comes next. On their website *www.quarterlifecrisis.com*, they cite the FAQ that "*Essentially, it is taking longer to become an adult today based on traditional markers such as financial independence and starting a family. The average American job hops 8 times before the age of 32, the average college graduate accrues $20,000 in education loan debt, and the average age to get married is now 27.*" If it is any comfort, this book and website let you know that you are not alone. What you are or will be going through is "normal" (hope that helps).

I've already written in the last chapter about how waiting can be a constructive time of discernment and re-orientation. Knowing that there will be figurative rapids and discerning your best course through or around the rapids are both elements of the grace found in times of waiting and in times of struggle. By now I hope you are discerning once again that the struggles and doubts and confusion that you are or will be facing is normal and if used well, can be times of deepening and growth (see *Liminal*). You are not the only one feeling the things you are feeling or asking the questions that you are asking.

Exponential Nothing

The disciples had come down from the mountain top and through the valley. They then returned to the upstairs room and found a way to wait for whatever was coming. They lived in the midst of prayerful conversations and prayerful waiting. Luke's brief passages in Acts don't really give us a clear time frame for this period of waiting. In Christian tradition it falls into another forty day period which is celebrated in the Christian calendar. Yet we're really not sure how long the small community of Jesus' followers remained in Jerusalem gathering there at the Upstairs Room and waiting for "what comes next". The next thing we learn from the text is that Peter seems to have pulled himself together enough to resume his leadership role. We read, *"In those days Peter stood up among the believers"*. We also find out that while they have been waiting and apparently doing nothing, somehow the number of believers had grown *"(together the crowd numbered about one hundred and twenty people)"*. It is perhaps simply some convenient editorializing by a scribe somewhere along the way, but for our purposes it represents another significant lesson from the story of the disciples at this very early point in their post-ascension ministry. The lesson - growth can and does happen while it might appear that you are "doing nothing".

In fact from eleven or so to one hundred twenty is not simply some growth, these numbers basically represent exponential growth. Exponential growth occurs when the growth rate of a mathematical function is proportional to the function's current value. There are 11 disciples and the next thing we know there are 11x11 believers = 120 (okay it should actually be 121 but who is counting?) At some point along the way, as the text comes to us today, someone felt that it was important to add that even before Pentecost the community of believers was growing. Growing nearly exponentially at that! Even before really getting the push of the Holy Spirit, the disciples seemed to be doing that which Jesus had charged them to do, "spread and live the gospel so that others might believe." Something was happening in the midst of doing nothing.

Apparently "while doing nothing" as they lived together in and around the upstairs room, in a neighborhood just outside the walls of Jerusalem, the disciples were making connections with others. While waiting for the Holy Spirit, their lives and their story were connecting with the lives and stories of others with whom their daily "doing nothing" lives came into relationship. While just living, just being, these relationships apparently developed to such a point that commitments were made and choices taken to believe, to join, and to follow. I love this part of the story. This part of the story is probably often overlooked. However, it is very significant because it highlights how God is so very present and active in these between times, in these times we feel like we're "doing nothing".

Think about your college and high school friends. Think about your Anam Cara if you have one/some. I imagine that these relationships that mean so much to you were not necessarily planned rather they just kind of happened. I've got a saying that my students and those I work with probably get tired of hearing, "Programs are the excuse for relationships to happen. God is present in and through relationships, not programs". This reminds me that making the space for relationships to happen is the most important aspect of my ministry. We can plan the most elaborate programs and events, but if relationships don't have time to develop and deepen in the midst of these programs then they are not worth the effort, time, and money. Churches often are clueless about this. They are clueless especially when it involves youth, students and young adults. Church folk mistakenly think that programs are the most important part of their ministry. However I have learned that programs are just the vehicle, the context, the excuse for the truly important things which are the relationships that are formed. Remember the focus here is on the being, rather than the doing.

Your deepest friendships probably grew while you were "doing nothing". They evolved while you were "hanging out" or while you were getting from here to there. Relationships happen while *being* more often than *doing*. So while you are feeling like you are "doing nothing", you might consider more intentionally how your "being with others" while "doing nothing" is actually "doing something" that can be significant and meaningful. (You may want to read that last sentence through a few times.) If you are open and aware and intentional, this time in your life can be a very important time of creating community and developing networks.

We've already covered the fact that your friends from college are spread all around the country and perhaps the world. It is very possible that you are in a job that you really don't like,

91

living in an apartment complex with people you don't have time to get to know, or living at home with people who don't really know you anymore, and you aren't really into going and hanging out at bars all by yourself. What you are thinking right now is... "There just isn't that much to work with, Tommy. Can you give me something to create with right now?" Why yes I can. I propose that your perception may once again be skewed.

I hope no one ever lied to you and said that this time in your life was going to be easy. I certainly won't. College was relatively easy. This is going to take more intentionality, more creativity, and more adjustment in your perceptions of what and who is important.

Checking Connections

Father Jack Hickey, who was the founder of Dismas House where I eventually worked following college, based the ministry on the simple concept of community. This concept is central to the ongoing mission of Dismas as stated in the mission statement as found on the website (www.dismas.org):

> *The mission of Dismas is to facilitate the reconciliation of former prisoners to society and society to former prisoners through development of a supportive community characterized by:*
>
> ❑ *Students and former prisoners living together in a family setting.*
> ❑ *The active involvement of volunteers from the broader community.*
> ❑ *A spirit of open and participative decision making and sharing across the Dismas network, with an emphasis on the common good.*

As I remember learning the concept from Father Jack, and eventually from my own experiences so many years ago, among the many reasons that people end up in prison is that they have little or no sense of connection to community. They perceive themselves as islands. Through their lives and often through a

92

series of broken relationships with others, they have become isolated. They perceive through their broken lenses that nothing they do has consequence or impact on others because their walls of isolation permit no one to have an impact on them. Therefore in committing crimes they perceive no victim because in their perception others do not matter. When caught and convicted, more often than not, society responds to this isolation and disconnection by further isolating them in prison with other isolated individuals. Prisons are gatherings of isolated individuals all of whom have broken concepts of connection, community, and consequence. Brokenness begets brokenness.

The Dismas communities seek to break the cycle of broken community by bringing these persons into "family", an interdependent system or community. This re-establishment of connection within community develops in stages. First there is the relationship between Dismas staff (which was my role) and the person while they are yet in prison. Through repeated prison visits a prospective resident develops a relationship with someone from the house even prior to their release. Once out of prison the individual is welcomed into the family, the community of the house including others coming out of prison and students who are also house residents. Just as with many family systems, the resident relationships are often complex and sometimes conflicted. Yet through intentional time in "family meetings" and in shared responsibility for the wellness of the community, each begins to understand and acknowledge the interdependence in the system. Finally there are the community volunteers who come regularly into the house becoming extended members of the "family system". Through these relationships especially, the residents gain the network and connections outside of the immediate family that support and help them find work and "success" as they eventually move out of Dismas and move further into life well lived. Basically stated, Dismas is about helping discover and connect with concentric circles of community.

Drawing of Circles of Community

Those of us blessed with relatively healthy family systems (and I realize that this is a big working assumption) tend to understand innately that our actions have consequence positively or negatively outside of ourselves. We have had opportunities to learn and experience within our own families and within our circle of friends how mutual accountability and forgiveness enables relationships to be sustained while negotiating conflicts and complexities. This is basic in social and moral development. At some point in our development we were taught and were able to comprehend and apply basic moral lessons that enable us to function within our relationships, our communities, and our society in general. If you have come from such a relatively healthy family system it is probably difficult for you to comprehend why and how individuals would become so isolated as to commit crimes worthy of society's condemnation, separation, and imprisonment.

In a similar way it is difficult for those of us who have been blessed to live western culture, especially the U.S. and to benefit from being (at least relatively speaking at the "top of the heap"), to comprehend what it means to struggle and to suffer at least in economic terms. Only 1% of the world's population has the opportunity to get a college education. Even in this country your prospective completion of your college education puts you in a relatively select group. College is a path to privilege and success, perhaps not as surely as it once was, yet it remains a path to opportunities rarely available to those who do not graduate at your level.

Yet again, following graduation you may find yourself where you never expected to be and hope that you will not be for long. You are relatively poor, you are relatively under-employed, you are relatively ill-housed, and you are relatively alone. *What a great time to connect with the rest of the world!* What a great time to discern and discover what is truly valuable. Consider yourself blessed! Jesus said in his Sermon on the Mount (paraphrased), "when you are poor, meek, mourning, hungry, thirsty, and even persecuted – You are blessed!" Not exactly what you were planning is it?

In the United States and much of the developed world, we define success much like the Merriam-Webster Dictionary definitions: *a favorable or desired outcome; also: the attainment of wealth, favor, or eminence: one that succeeds.* In other words, the successful

94

person is the one who makes it to the top of the heap (eminence) with the most stuff (wealth). Obviously "blessed" according to Jesus is very different from "success" as our culture defines it. That success may be out there for you somewhere. But from the point from graduation, especially if you find yourself struggling to make it economically, you can consider yourself blessed.

You are welcome to use this with your parents or others who may pressure you to "succeed". Tell them that you are going to put off success for a while and just make the most of your blessings. (Cool, huh?)

You're Blessed

So here are my beatitudes for recent middle/upper-middle class college graduates:

- *Blessed are you when you are working an entry level job* - because you can get to know hard working people who might not have had the same kind of opportunities as you. You can get to know the cleaning staff, the maintenance staff, the truck drivers, the administrative assistants, etc.... You can learn from and develop relationships with these people who are among the "working class" in our society.

- *Blessed are you when you struggle to afford rent* – because you can perhaps value the roof over your head and understand how tenuous the line between home and homelessness is in reality for so many in this nation and the world.

- *Blessed are you when you struggle to afford groceries* – because you might identify more with those who struggle daily with hunger who have no way of knowing where their next meal will come.

- *Blessed are you when you are lonely* – because you might more deeply appreciate your friends and family.

- *Blessed are you when you can't afford something and you must choose* – because you might find value in the simple and

95

affordable things in life, learning that value is different from cost.

◻ *Blessed are you when you shop at thrift stores* – because you can find great stuff and good prices, discovering how much money you have wasted at the mall.

◻ *Blessed are you when you are fired or let-go from your job* – because you will learn all the lessons under even more critical circumstances.

◻ *Blessed are you when you feel like you failed* – because you can learn more from failure than you can from easy success.

There is opportunity in each of these struggles and it is through taking full advantage of each opportunity that you will discover the blessings in each. I can't tell you exactly how to make the most of the blessings hidden in your struggles. But I can tell you that each of the blessings hidden in your post college struggles will be meaningless if you are not open to receive them. I can also tell you that they will be meaningless in the long-term if you forget the lessons of your struggles in years to come.

Among the best ways that I can recommend as a way to learn and grow through your struggles is to find partners. Find a person or persons to go through the struggles with you. Think of the TV shows I mentioned in Chapter 2, or even better think *Office Space* (one of the classic twenty-something movies of all time) and the dude next door. Unlike your college friends or your Anam Cara, these friends in the midst of struggle/blessings might just be short-term relationships. After all, you are in the midst of transitional times and your relationships in this period may or may not be long term. It doesn't matter. Make connections anyway, especially if you find someone with whom you can identify with in the midst of your struggle. These people will be like fellow passengers on a life-boat or fellow victims of a disaster. You can make connection with these folks simply on the basis of how much you hate your job, or how tired you are of eating spaghetti and sauce every night, or how desperate you are for cheap entertainment, etc.… . Even if you know it might only be for weeks or months go ahead and make the connection. Take a chance on the friendship. At least you will have someone to hang out with while you commiserate together.

In the list of beatitudes, I also mentioned other connections you should make during this valley time in your young life. This may be the only time in your life that you have the unique opportunity to immerse yourself in another culture for an extended period of time. It is still the case that a majority of four year college graduates in this country come from the middle and upper middle class in this country (and this is admittedly my intended audience). Yet at this time following college you may intentionally or unintentionally find yourself living in the midst of working class or even near poverty circumstances. Great! Make the most of this opportunity as well. Get to know your neighbors, get to know the folks who work at the shops and stores nearby, get to know the retired folks, get to know the homeless folks, and get to know the children. Immerse yourself as much as possible in the community you find yourself in.

Also at your job or jobs, get to know the folks who haven't had the opportunity that you once took for granted (your college education). Get to know the people who really produce the goods and services in the economy. If you are in health care, get to know the orderlies, nurses, and other support staff. If you are in business, get to know the drivers, cleaners, and administrative assistants. Where ever you find yourself while you are close to the bottom rung of the "career ladder", get to know and value the folks who are there with you. There is wisdom there.

Among the times in my life when I discovered the value of getting to know the folks in support roles was during the four years that I served as Associate Pastor with Youth and Their Families at First Presbyterian Church in Greensboro. This is a large congregation of approximately 3500 at the time, with a staff of over sixty persons in various roles. I came to this role from my prior role as camp director at Cedar Ridge in Louisville, Kentucky. As camp director my responsibilities included doing anything that needed to be done; setting up tables, stacking chairs, mopping floors, cleaning toilets, cooking meals, repairing broken plumbing, etc.... So when I came to First Presbyterian and found myself a part of a large staff with specific designated roles, it was hard for me to let go of the "grunt work" that I had always done. I seldom saw my job and their job rather I saw our job that needed to be done.

The housekeeping and maintenance staff took note that this new pastor didn't hesitate to work for a living. So fairly quickly these folks realized that I was easy to get to know and so they let me get to know them. Among these good folks is Franklin Brown who is the long serving director of housekeeping at First Presbyterian Greensboro. Franklin isn't an ordained minister, but his ministry of hospitality and his graciousness in all things is a model of Christ's Gospel. He is such a model that I regularly had middle school confirmands connect with Franklin during their training and learn how he is among the Saints of the Church. There are many others on the "support staff" at FPCG who live the Gospel daily in what they do behind the scenes. When I return to the Church for a Presbytery meeting or other event, ten years later I still make sure that I reconnect with these good folks, for they were and are my friends and companions through that part of my journey.

Once again as you find yourself in your post-college challenges, you may not be in these places or in your jobs for very long. Yet I strongly encourage you to connect as much as possible to the communities and the people where you find yourself even if temporarily. There are mentors and guides among the "support staff" who can teach you more about life and about what is really important than many of your professors in college. Your neighbors in that crummy apartment might become your best friends at least for a while. So take the time to make connections within whatever community you find yourself. Who knows, you might find just what you were looking for all the time.

A Brief Word about Intentional Mission Years

One can find themselves in a cultural immersion experience unintentionally as I describe above or intentionally through a year or multiple year intentional mission experience. Whether through the Peace Corps, Americorps, PCUSA Young

98

Adult Volunteers, Episcopal Service Corps, Teach for America, or any number of volunteer programs, I strongly encourage folks coming out of college to consider participation in such programs. These intentional cultural immersion/mission programs will usually provide young adults a guided process of discernment through challenge and reflection. Even if you have had a semester or a year of study abroad and have perhaps traveled extensively in other cultures, I encourage you to consider a year in a service and/or mission program.

You do not have to travel abroad for very valuable immersion experiences. Nearly anywhere in the United States you can find opportunities to serve within a very different and challenging cultural setting. The important element of any such experience is an intentional process of learning and reflection. I also think that it is very important that the participant be open to cultural diversity, open to connect and develop relationships with the people in the community, and open to the learning of many types that will surely be available.

Throughout my years in ministry with youth and young adults I have led numerous short-term mission experiences. Though very valuable learning opportunities, these cannot match the challenges and growth which come through a long-term opportunity. This is why I have always been an advocate for such opportunities. Just as with my own summer in Southeast Alaska and my Vista year with Dismas House, young adults can learn lessons about themselves and others that they will draw on for the rest of their lives. They may also connect and develop relationships that remain important throughout their lives. Keep an eye out for Anam Cara.

Relationship Development Studies and Practice Major

If the disciples had been paying attention (which they must have occasionally done), they may have noticed without really even trying that while it seems they were "doing nothing" they were actually beginning to do what Jesus had charged them to do. "Go and make disciples". I think Jesus might as well have said, 'live intentionally, live gracefully, live the Gospel I have shared with you, live in relationship with one another, live open to relationships with others, live open to God, and disciples will come be a part of what you are being. Basically being in relationship with one another, with God and making relationships with others had become their full-time gig. Apparently they were doing well even before they were charged up by the Holy Spirit at Pentecost.

Wouldn't that be a great profession? Your job is to make friends with people, make connections with people, make connections with God and with creation, and you can make a living doing it. Actually in some ways I think that is the gist of my job and many of us in ministry. I actually think that this is the gist of many jobs if you really think about it. Yet I have never seen a college major called *Relationship Development Studies and Practice*. Yet isn't that what we're all really majoring in one way or another? That is unless you find contentment as a major in *Isolation and Disconnection Studies and Practice* (there are those who do). Relationship development is something that we all do for a "living" whether we are introverts or extroverts. As human beings we live in family, we live in community, we live in groups, and we live in connection and relationship with one another. Yet in most cases, unless there is a relationship crisis, we tend not to attend to relationships intentionally.

Developmentally speaking this is appropriate. Human development theorists have posited that human social development progresses through stages just as cognitive, emotional, and moral development progress. According to these developmental theories the socio-emotional task of young adults 18-35 is to seek intimacy and solidarity as opposed to isolation. In this stage you are supposed to be "looking for love" and you are supposed to be *majoring in relationship development* in regards to life partner and intimate friendships. During our college years relationships are certainly a focus, but they are one focus among so many. In the midst of hundreds of potential relationships, with so many friends just down the hall, we may tend to take this relationship development task for granted. Once you've graduated, once friends and potential partners have scattered, once the reality of isolation becomes real, now you can really focus on the task at hand.

Therefore this time following college is an excellent time for you to apply yourself to your unofficial post-college major in *Relationship Development Studies and Practice*. Now that your friends and potential partners have scattered this major will be more challenging. But you should be able to focus well - after all you have completed your degree work. Now you can really become a student of life. Now you can attend fully to a study and practice of how you relate to others, how you connect with others, and how to more fully develop your skills and gain practical experience in relationships. It is even better if your job is just a job and not a career. Because instead of multi-tasking like you did in college, you can actually uni-task. For once in your life you can focus on the "one thing." You too can become a Relationship Development Studies and Practice major at the *Life-Long Learning College of Human Existence.* Among the great thing about this post-college degree is that that there won't be grades or tests, beyond the ones you give or set for you.

Here are some of the reasons why now may be a great time to work on your *Relationships Development Studies and Practice Major:*

◻ You've got nothing better to do...
◻ You are over 21 now and that is a big difference from 18 in more ways than one...
◻ You have interactions with people other than college students or professors... .
◻ You need something constructive to tell your parents...
◻ You are done with drama...
◻ You might as well critique yourself, everyone else is...

Recommended Course of Study:
Relationship Development Studies and Practice Majors – Non-Degree Track*

Pre-requisite/Review Courses
Basic Human Development Theory – *in this course you will review the work of Piaget, Erickson, Kohlberg, Fowler and others to gain a working knowledge of human development theory.*
Adolescent Tasks Competency and Completion – *in this course you will consider your progress on adolescent development tasks. This course will especially focus on hampered self-esteem, latent narcissism, and complex reasoning. Continued review and/or therapy may be recommended.*

101

Required Courses

Family of Origin – *in this course you will explore and analyze the relationships in your family of origin. Special focus will be given to the strengths, values, and roles learned as well as the issues of potential struggle including re-negotiation of adult parent to young adult child relationship.*

Personal Relationship History – *in this course you will examine your history of relationships both intimate and non-intimate - seeking to discern the positive, negative, neutral impact of these relationships and patterns that may have emerged. Special focus will be given to periods of conflict and patterns of conflict resolution and/ or avoidance.*

Intimate Relationship Studies and Analysis – *this course is a preparation for successful long-term partner relationships such as marriage. In this course you will study and analyze successful and failed long-term committed relationships with which you are familiar. You will explore traits and talents you might offer to a successful intimate relationship, traits in which you may be lacking, and methods and strategies for developing required traits.*

The Holy Other – *this course explores your relationship with The Holy Other (what many name as God). In this course you will explore your image of God and analyze how this image or images impacts your relationship with others individually and communally.*

Current Relational Status Review and Analysis – *in this course you will review your current relationships with co-workers, friends, family, and intimates. You will analyze these relationships and seek to discern how each might remain or become more mutually constructive and contributive.*

Sex and the Soul – *in this course you will explore the integrative reality of human sexuality and human spirituality. You will explore how western culture tends to compartmentalize sex and sexuality from spirituality, emotionality, and the intellect. In this course you will seek to more fully integrate your sexual self and your spiritual self in an effort to bring your whole integrated self into all of your relationships.*

Electives

Global Perspectives on Relationship Studies – *in this class you will explore the dynamics of relationship in the global context as well as the varied expressions of human relationships throughout the world.*

102

Rites of Passages – *in this class you will examine rites and ritual of passage throughout human history and will discover and experience passages you might have missed in your own life.*

Of course I am not necessarily suggesting that you literally do this actual course work. Regrettably few of these courses of study are offered or are affordable for those who might most benefit, meaning those at the appropriate developmental stage. What I am suggesting is that you take the time while you have the time to think through each of these "courses". While "doing nothing" do something that might have benefits for the long term. If you work well with written resources, find some good books that might be your guides. If you work well in conversation with others, find a trusted mentor or guide who can do this course work with you. If you work best alone, keep a journal and take a week or more to focus on each topic. However you choose to begin your course work, make an effort while you have the time to begin. Now is a good time to begin and there really isn't a term for completion.

This is not a degree program from which you or anyone else ever really graduates. Relationship development studies and practice truly is *lifelong learning.* However through your intentional practice, study, and experience each of us can certainly become a teacher/mentor/practitioner/instructor in this field.

Working the Network

Checking your connections, considering your blessings, majoring in relationships, suddenly doing all this "nothing" is getting to be a lot of effort. That's the thing I pray that you are beginning to realize about this *unscripted* time that you are in or getting ready to head into. This can be a time of learning, discerning, growing and becoming. God didn't leave the Israelites in the wilderness for forty years because there wasn't a good trail from Egypt to the Promised Land. In one of the core stories from Judeo-Christian scripture, God uses the Exodus to teach, to guide, to create, and to connect the people with God and with one another. In the midst of the wilderness journey, in the midst of sharing the Ten Commandments, God through Moses shares the purpose for these commands. In so doing God shares the why and wherefore for the struggles of the wilderness journey, for the conditions of the relationship, for the requirements of the covenant stated in Deuteronomy 6 verse 3, *"that it may be well with you"*.

It isn't for God's sake that we struggle, that we encounter difficulties, that we sometimes wander in the wilderness wondering how to live or what comes next? Through these challenges, we learn, discern, grow and become more fully ourselves. *So that it might be well with us*; so that we might be more wholly, more fully ourselves. I think that many are confused about this point especially in our western culture filled with promises of false fulfillment and momentary happiness. "That it may be well with you" is not a promise of happiness, but rather of wellness and of wholeness. Bringing your full self in relationship with others and with God comes through a process of struggle, a journey through several wildernesses, and the learning, discerning, growing and becoming that usually only happens as a result of such experiences.

Isn't it therefore a great thing that you are either in or heading into such a time? If done well and with intention, creativity, adaptation, improvisation, consciousness and awareness, in and through your journey in this unscripted time you can become more you!

The Disciples Finally Get It!!!

In those forty days between the Ascension and Pentecost and in those forty years of wandering in the Wilderness the network of God's intention (that it may be well with us) was being strengthened. Without their teacher, Jesus, the disciples became more interdependent upon one another. Through the Exodus journey the people of Israel became more inter-dependent. They became networked and connected one to another and all with God. In your transitional time I have encouraged you to consider your connections, your family, your friends, your co-workers, etc.... I have recommended a course of study, of reflection on how you relate to all of these persons including your intimate relationships. It may seem that I have guided you to look inward; perhaps I have.

However my purpose is to help you consider not your co-dependence but rather your inter-dependence. In other words, your inward journey during this transitional period is not about you and your selfish needs. This isn't about what you get from these relationships, meeting your needs and desires alone, getting you further along the path towards success as defined by the West. Instead your inward reflection and quest to consider will hopefully lead you beyond yourself, towards higher levels of consciousness, awareness, and intentionality for the sake of the world. This is where all true wilderness journeys tend to lead. The deeper one discerns him/herself the more one discovers that which is beyond, it leads to the other, other creatures, other humans, and ultimately it leads to God.

I think that in their time prayerfully waiting while living, the disciples in that Upstairs Room were in the midst of their own wilderness experience. Our clue is that anytime forty days or forty years is referenced we are to make the connection with a transformative wilderness experience. Their time in this place was not in isolation or desolation; rather it was more like the intentional course of study detailed earlier. With sharper understanding, they could now reflect on all that Jesus had taught, all that he had done, all the experiences and struggles they had come through. Now living in this community of disciples integrated by gender, age, agenda, gifts, etc... they could learn to live *well* in the deepest sense of meaning. I think in these forty days – the disciples finally Get It! Now they are ready to receive the Holy Spirit and begin to do *what* it is they were created, gifted and taught to do. Now is their time!

Your *When*

Have you noticed that in this chapter about *wondering when* I have spent much of it writing about relationships? Even when I write about *growing while doing nothing* the thing it seems you are supposed to be growing is relationships with others. Even the course of study that I recommend is almost exclusively focused on relationships. Isn't *when* about timing? Well you are forgetting the image in the first several lines of our passage from scripture. Remember that back up on the mountaintop, the disciples where asking about timing (when would the Kingdom of Israel be restored?) and Jesus told them that this timing was not their concern. That is God stuff. Rather their task was to receive the power of Holy Spirit and to witness in Jerusalem, Judea, Samaria and to the whole earth. See how their when (timing) question gets answered with a when (relational) response. There is the twist (surprised?) When is not about time but rather about relationship.

So when you open yourself to others, when you let go and let God, when you realize you are blessed surrounded by and perhaps one of the least of these, when you are aware of your connection and inter-dependence with others, when it is well with you, then you begin to get it. *Then is when.*

> Do you get it?
> If not, go back and read the chapter once again.
> So now we have found
> Your where,
> Your who,
> Your how,
> Your what,
> And your when.
> All that is left is why.
> I bet you have already guessed.
> Why?
> Because.

Chapter 6
Wondering *Why?*

Why Questions

During challenging times in our lives, like the one you may soon find yourself entering, it is appropriate to ask *why questions*. You have revised your resume', updated your references, and practiced your interviewing techniques. No one seems to be hiring. "Why can't I get a good job?" You have done everything that you are supposed to have done, gotten your undergraduate degree, working a low paying, but regular job, and you've stopped drinking as much beer. "Why are my parents always treating me like a kid?" You have gone to coffee shops, gone to bars, even gone to a young-adult mixer at church. "Why can't I find any friends?" You have lost some weight, changed the way you wear your hair, you even went on a few blind dates. "Why can't I find a good guy?"

Why may be the most asked question during this time in your life, though often you can't even bring yourself to ask it out-loud? You convince yourself that you are okay and that you aren't really that concerned about things. You realize this transition from college to whatever comes next is pretty challenging. There are a lot of people who don't have jobs even as good as the crappy one you have. Many people don't know where their next meal is coming from and you still have access to the folks' refrigerator. You really shouldn't complain. You still have friends, though it is difficult to connect sometimes. You are a little lonely, but it is a good time to learn how to be content with yourself. Things could be worse, much worse. But to be honest, there are times when you have cried yourself to sleep and others when you get really mad and just want to scream, *"Why does life have to be so damn hard? Why, Why, Why?"*

Difficult Choices

Even though it seems that the disciples are getting things figured out and even Peter is beginning to re-assert himself as a leader of the group, this group of Jesus' followers pretty quickly faces some difficult decisions and choices. During their community building in the upstairs room, they seem to have determined a few things. Since there are now eleven chosen disciples (meaning those who will take the gospel on the road) and that doesn't divide well into the 2 by 2 that Jesus instructed, they need to choose someone from among their larger company to replace Judas. Oh yeah, Judas. That's the other issue about which they seem to need to come to terms. What is to be said about Judas?

Here is how Luke writes about these things in Acts:

> In those days Peter stood up among the believers (a group numbering about a hundred and twenty) and said, "Brothers and sisters, the Scripture had to be fulfilled in which the Holy Spirit spoke long ago through David concerning Judas, who served as guide for those who arrested Jesus. He was one of our number and shared in our ministry." "For," said Peter, "it is written in the Book of Psalms: "May his place be deserted; let there be no one to dwell in it,' and, "May another take his place of leadership.' Therefore it is necessary to choose one of the men who have been with us the whole time the Lord Jesus was living among us, beginning from John's baptism to the time when Jesus was taken up from us. For one of these must become a witness with us of his resurrection." So they nominated two men: Joseph called Barabbas (also known as Justus) and Matthias. Then they prayed, "Lord, you know everyone's heart. Show us which of these two you have chosen to take over this apostolic ministry, which Judas left to go where he belongs." Then they cast lots, and the lot fell to Matthias; so he was added to the eleven apostles.

The Judas question has been a challenging issue for Christians ever since the first days of the church. Was Judas doing God's will and therefore is he to be honored for having the courage of his convictions or was he criminal, deceitful and cowardly, therefore deserving of torment and suffering at the lowest level of Hell? Bet you can guess which one we've gone with for most of Church history. Yep the torment and suffering, you betcha! Much of this has to do with this passage from Acts and a nice little textual addition from sometime centuries after Luke, which I didn't include in the passage above. This textual addition explains the information about the barren and deserted place which Judas bought with his ill-gotten sum and then goes on to add some spilled blood and guts as well. (Go ahead dig up verses 18 & 19 if you need to see it for yourself.) Yet many remain unsatisfied with Judas' role in all this. Why did God need Judas (or Jesus for that matter) to be a scapegoat? Why did Jesus call Judas and train him as one of the Twelve if he knew that this same Judas would betray him?

We really don't have the space to dig into these questions here, but suffice it to say that these why questions, like most why questions remain essentially unanswered, at least in the factual sense. There have been piles of books written containing hundreds of theories in response to these and related questions. Yet the question of why remains.

Here is my theory on the matter. It makes for a great story because every good story needs a villain, someone to blame. We can't blame God for Jesus' death that becomes way too complicated when you get into the dynamics of Trinitarian doctrine. We can't blame the Romans because that is just too easy. For centuries Christians blamed the Jews, but that is too easy and anti-Semitic. So we look around for someone to blame. Judas! Good old Judas. Let's blame it on him.

Just a side note before we delve further into how we perceive Judas still today. I wonder how these people who really knew Judas as a human being felt about losing their friend and companion? I think a twinge of this slips through in the passage when it says, *He was one of our number and shared in our ministry.* Perhaps on that journey through the graveyard, they thought of their lost friend Judas. Now let's get back to the blame and guilt.

Reading Backwards

Have you ever noticed that because of this part of the story about Judas' guilt that in all of the plays, musicals, performances about Jesus and the disciples there is always this negative energy in the portrayal of Judas? Who wants to play the part of Judas? It is always the dark and brooding types. Judas is never portrayed as a happy, positive person. He has come down through Church, literary, and theatrical history as kind of creepy, the hard core Goth of his time. So let me ask you this, why did Jesus choose him to be one of the Twelve? Much less why did Jesus apparently give him the responsibility of keeping track of the funds for this whole enterprise? It seems like we are doing that old trick of perspective. We are reading the story through the lens of the ending. Author, speaker, and friend Brian McLaren (*www.brianmclaren.net*) re-introduced me to this concept at a recent conference. Since we know how the story ends, we interpret the character of Judas from that one perspective (he is creepy and kills himself), rather than interpreting the character and the story as it flows from start to finish.

We have a tendency to do just this, to judge by the ending so to speak. This can get us in trouble in so many ways. Go back to the why questions asked in the first paragraph from this chapter. *"Why can't I get a good job?" "Why are my parents always treating me like a kid?" "Why can't I find any friends?" "Why can't I find a good guy?"* Take a moment. What do you notice about all of these questions?

Each of these questions is filled with assumptions, judgments, interpretations, and negative energy. *"Why can't I get a good job?"* for example assumes that you can't get a good job rather than assuming that you just haven't found a good job yet. This question judges your situation from the assumed ending of failure. *"Why are my parents always treating me like a kid?"* as another example, may be based on one or two instances where one's parents may have responded to less than mature behavior or actually been disrespectful of one's growth and development. But *always*, really, in every interaction they treat you like you are 7 or 8 years old? Once again there is a judgment made where an assumed ending or result is always the case. This rearview lens is providing a skewed view of your present and your future. Check your language and how you are describing your life. You may be judging yourself and assuming that the life you are living now will be your life for the foreseeable future.

One of the things that I say often to students when they are struggling with a difficulty is, "Now is not for always." I mean by this that the situation and difficulties with which they are struggling will change. Either they will find a way through their struggles or various factors in their life will change and the pain and struggle they currently feel will become less and less until it doesn't impact them in any noticeable ways.

Be careful about judging in general but especially try to avoid judging your own future from your present position or worse your present position from an assumed failed future. Perhaps this can be called the Judas dilemma, using a negative outcome to skew the entire retrospective of one's life.

Again this may seem like a contradiction of the futuring materials I shared earlier in the book. However, the futuring techniques I shared do not assume a future, but rather create scenarios for possible futures based on trend analysis and adaptation and orientation in the midst of various change factors. There is no judgment involved, only possibilities. Retrospect does not come into play except in the analysis of trends.

Chances Are

Having explored how the disciples of that time and Christians throughout history have viewed Judas, let's look and see what might be learned through this business of choosing his replacement.

This little story offers some very interesting insight into the story of the disciples. First it tells us that there were more than the Twelve that we always talk about and often assume were the only ones hanging out with Jesus as he taught, preached, and camped his way through Palestine. Apparently a fair number of people were part of that little tribe including these two who are given the opportunity to join the chosen Twelve. Matthias and this guy with three names, "*Joseph called Barabbas (also known as Justus)*". (Come on Luke were you trying to please everyone in the retelling of this story? He ends up losing, so what was so important?)   Anyway, here is where some must get the idea that God chooses sides in games of chance or in sports.   The disciples cast lots which means basically that they threw dice.   They offered a prayer asking for God's decision to be shown through however the dice fell.   This was apparently a common decision making practice at the time?   Notice that in their prayer they also stuck it to Judas one more time.   Then they cast and the lot fell to Matthias.

Besides the obvious lesson that in all important decisions one should cast lots (Just joking), there is the intriguing lesson about chance or fate or whatever one wants to call things totally beyond our control and the role this plays in our lives.

To explore this story further I would like for you to put yourself in Joseph Barabbas Justus' shoes.   Here you are with the opportunity to get this promotion.   You really feel like you deserve the position because you have been loyal to this company all along. You have supported the team at all the important events. Remember it was you who really found the kid with the loaf of bread and two fish at the feeding the five thousand festival. During these last forty days or so, you have really pulled your weight renegotiating the lease on the Upstairs Room with the landlord. He really wanted the group out, but you negotiated the original grief clause that stipulates a forty day period of mourning following any death wherein the group is permitted to remain. You really think that confirms it.   They have to choose you! Matthias is great and all, but you are gifted!

Then it comes to the actual decision and they cast lots? Really, you guys are going to leave this one up to chance?   Oh yeah, say a prayer and make it God's decision, like one can argue with that.   Here they go and it falls on... Matthias.

Have you ever been on the hiring end of a job interview? I have had a few chances to plow through resume' after resume' and interview after interview.   Then I sat down with a team and discussed the merits of one candidate over another.   Sometimes it is pretty clear.   One person is a perfect match for the position. However, I have also been in the position of really having to choose between two fairly even candidates.   One would bring this set of great strengths to the position and the other would bring different but also very fine attributes. How do you choose, the first one to return your call or the one who laughs at the stupidest joke during the final interview? Which one gets the job?

I know it is really hard on the other side to put together resume' after resume' and go to interview after interview. Worse yet, it is even more difficult to receive so many rejection letters in the mail. However, as this story shows sometimes it is up to chance or it is up to God. Whichever you want to believe is fine. Both are out of your control.

The important thing to remember is that if you have done everything that you can to position yourself for a job, or a date, or an apartment, or a grad school and it doesn't come through for you, very often it isn't about you. It may be something beyond your control. So don't take it personally. Why didn't you get the job, or the date, or the apartment or into that grad school? Who knows? Perhaps it was just chance or a role of the dice. Perhaps it was God? Why? Because.

Why? Because

Do you know that college myth about the philosophy course? The professor asks one question on the final exam, why? Students write pages and pages filled with philosophical concepts responding to various questions of why humanity exists, why humans struggle, why there is evil in the world, etc.... However one student simply responds with the word *because*. She gets a perfect score on the test and everyone else fails. The point of this story is not that the professor was a complete jerk. The point is that because often *because* really does answer the question why just as well as any other answer and sometimes better.

Because can answer the question *Why* in a somewhat satisfying way but it requires breaking the word down into its component parts. *Be* is a great little word. It is the core of Hamlet's wondering, "To be or not to be." To *BE* is to exist, to be present, and to take up space, to be a collection of organized matter. In a human sense to *Be* is to be human, matter organized into a sentient form which is recognized as a human being.

Cause is also a wonderful word. *Cause* is the initial action. *Cause* is to engage. In looking back one can determine the *Cause* of

113

or the initiating action an event. Mrs. O'Leary's cow kicking over a candle *caused* the Great Chicago Fire. *Cause* can also be purpose. One can do something for a *cause*. *Because* works because it not only answers the question adequately without implying or inferring further questions, but it also goes deeper in a philosophical sense. The statement *Because* answers the question *Why* because it basically says *a being engaged an action and therefore it was so*, simple cause and effect. I could go on and on (after all I am an English major). But I will stop there since you probably get the idea.

Remember when you were a child and you asked your parent 'why' and they answered 'because' and you would ask 'but why' and they would respond 'just because' and you would again ask 'but why' and they would tell you to be quiet? Remember how frustrating that felt? You didn't know it at the time, but what you were really asking was a deeper question. You wanted to know more than the basics of causality. You were wondering about intentionality. You knew innately that there must be an intention or purpose behind the cause and effect, the action and reaction, and therefore you were seeking a response that would satisfy the intention of your own question. You simply didn't know how to ask the question yet or perhaps your parent didn't know the answer.
Now you know how to ask your question. So ask it. What was the intention (or perhaps un-intention) behind the action that caused the effect? What thoughts or instinct or purpose did the actor (the be) have in taking the action (the cause) which resulted in the effect or circumstance and was it intentional or un-intentional. Who or what gets the blame or the credit for this happening? That is what we are really looking for when we ask the question why. We're looking to give credit or blame. (Hey Judas, we're looking for you again.)
We'll come back to that.

Be-the-cause

For now let's look more closely at the factor of intentionality and un-intentionality. As we have learned the *be* (actor) *causes* (engages) *something to happen* (action). But what is the

114

intention behind the engagement and the action? What was the thought, purpose, or instinct that initiated the movement that became the *because*? Most creatures, we have learned, act and respond instinctively most of the time. Only in more evolved creatures is there thought engaged at various levels in specific actions. This thought towards intentional action is an aspect of consciousness. Use of tools to accomplish something is a prime example. We humans at least lay claim to the highest level of consciousness and therefore can lay claim to the highest level of intentionality. In other words we can think about our actions and the resulting consequences or reactions. We have that choice to think about it. We don't always do so, but we do have this ability. Therefore we as beings can consciously choose to cause. We can be-the-cause.

It is this consciousness or unconsciousness in our being the cause which we interpret as intentionality or un-intentionality (which is why we can later give credit or lay blame).

As I have guided you on this journey from graduation to whatever comes next, my purpose has been for you to gain consciousness and awareness regarding the circumstances you find yourself in during this time following college. For much of your life you followed expectations (the script) at various levels of consciousness. As a child you were primarily reacting at an appropriate developmental level to the actions of others. During childhood you are learning more and more about action and consequence and gaining increasing consciousness about your ability to act and to cause. This is why until you were 18 years old society gives you a bit of a pass, implying that you are not fully conscious of your actions and the resulting consequences. However, now that you are twenty-something it is assumed that you are fully responsible for you actions and therefore liable for the credit or the blame of the resulting consequence. It is now assumed that you are a conscious actor. You can *be the cause*, whether you do so intentionally or un-intentionally is up to you. This is why now, after all these years; you get to write your own script.

One of the things that I have learned especially in the last few years is that *intentional behaviors beget intentional consequences, while un-intentional behaviors beget un-intentional consequences*. Intentional

115

behaviors derive from consciousness and conversely of course un-intentional behaviors derive from un-consciousness.

You might have some experience with intentional and/or un-intentional behaviors begetting intentional or un-intentional consequences. I think we all do. The important thing is that we learn from these and that these experiences help us to grow in consciousness and awareness of the ultimate inter-connectedness and inter-dependence of life.

Consider Judas once again. We can assume various things from the story we have about his intentions which guided his actions which eventually resulted in Jesus' crucifixion and therefore according to orthodox Christian belief resulted in the Salvation of humanity. But was that Judas' intention? Many scholars now assume that Judas' intention was to either save himself from the coming persecution or to rescue a movement in which he passionately believed. We really don't know his motivation or intention. From the story we learn that he was extremely upset with the initial results of his actions so therefore we can assume that there were un-intentional consequences resulting from un-intentional behaviors. However, we are looking at the story in reverse, so we can't really assume anything. Was Judas in control of his actions or was God? Again, who gets the credit or the blame?

Living your Life Consciously

I obviously don't know how your life is going to turn out. I have no idea about the specific challenges/opportunities you will encounter. However, I do know that the more conscious and engaged we are the more we can make intentional choices which can result in intentional consequences. I also know that there is truth in the inverse as well.

In this book we have journeyed from the mountaintop of graduation through the valleys of liminal space to the relative security of a third place and into the river rapids of struggles where we have found companions and guides who at the right time have taken us out into the bright day of consciousness and awareness.

116

This is not a journey that you take once in your life. It comes again and again and again at each stage of growth and development. Each time we take this journey, through all of the steps, we can discover more and more levels and channels of consciousness and awareness. I have shared this with you because there is no reason to wait until you are older to take this journey. Each time we learn more; therefore you can discover more than the person who went before – that's me.

The disciples were also our guides along the journey. I have followed the path that they trod in the scriptural story and perhaps in the literal story some nearly two-thousand years ago. I have learned a great deal in following their path, I hope you have as well.

So you now have your what, where, who, how, when and now why. All you need is to begin to live and write your script. I wish you the best and bless you on your journey of living your life.

Amazing things can happen when one person, a group of people, or groups of people begin to live their life and continue to live through all the stages of life with deep consciousness, awareness and intentionality. It can and has changed the world. That is where I will conclude. Considering what is possible.

Postscript

2 When the day of Pentecost came, they were all together in one place. ² Suddenly a sound like the blowing of a violent wind came from heaven and filled the whole house where they were sitting. ³ They saw what seemed to be tongues of fire that separated and came to rest on each of them. ⁴ All of them were filled with the Holy Spirit and began to speak in other tongues as the Spirit enabled them (Acts 2, NIV)

The promise of conscious living is evident in this passage from Acts 2. But first let's review the whole story and the process of becoming-the-cause that became Pentecost. For three years the chosen Twelve and the extended company of disciples had traveled with Jesus learning how to learn through the new lens of Jesus' teaching. Then they encountered the chaos of that week in Jerusalem which ended in Jesus' execution by the Roman authorities. According to the story, on the third day Jesus returned to them in a recognizable form and continued to teach for forty days (talk about a powerful object lesson!) Finally he ascended and left them with their assignment – Go and proclaim! Graduation day! Now it was time to commence their next steps. But wait, again according to tradition there was another journey of forty days in a figurative wilderness before they were ready to really begin to live their calling.

It is these forty days that we have journeyed through this book. It is through the significant process of these steps and stages through which the disciples become fully aware and conscious of the Holy Spirit. They become aware of this mysterious presence of God which has been in their midst all along. Only then when fully conscious and intentionally aware is the spirit of God revealed on the day we call Pentecost. The story says that on this day in some form of energy moving the Holy Spirit moved among them. We can interpret this as their awareness of God's Spirit became so real to them that it could now be consciously received, available, and accessible to each of them. Importantly it could also be sensed and shared with others.

Those last forty days "became the be-cause" that engaged a movement that has changed the world; that initiated the Christian faith; and that has significantly influenced and impacted humanity for the past two millennia. I propose that it is the process of applying what was learned in the previous three years in very practical and real ways, this small group of people intentionally began to follow Jesus' teachings, they began to share it with others, and most importantly began to live it. Therefore I propose that it is in these forty days that what we know as the Christian church was truly initiated. We mark the moment on Pentecost, but the process began forty days earlier.

Consider then how significant this time of transition from college graduation to whatever moment will mark the beginning of your next stage might become. As I mentioned in the introduction, the year following graduation was for me a very significant period of struggle, learning, and growth that has echoed loudly through the rest of my life. It certainly has not been the last significant period of struggle, growth and becoming in my life, nor was these forty days the last significant stage in the development and evolution of the Christian movement. Yet without that year I know that my life would be very different. I also suspect that without those forty days of wondering and wandering in and around the upstairs room, the group we know as the disciples might not have fully engaged the movement that became the church. At least not the image of the church that we find in Acts 2 verses 42-47:

> *42 They devoted themselves to the apostles' teaching and to fellowship, to the breaking of bread and to prayer. 43 Everyone was filled with awe at the many wonders and signs performed by the apostles. 44 All the believers were together and had everything in common. 45 They sold property and possessions to give to anyone who had need. 46*

Every day they continued to meet together in the temple courts. They broke bread in their homes and ate together with glad and sincere hearts, [47] praising God and enjoying the favor of all the people. And the Lord added to their number daily those who were being saved.

This is an image of an intentional, conscious and aware community of people living fully in relationship with one another and with God. It has been held up ever since as the model image of Christian community, though it has rarely if ever been fully realized. The most we get is a momentary glimpse, but this does not mean it can't be an idea towards which to strive. Just this glimpse has transformed lives and positively impacted millions of lives.

I am not suggesting that you will begin a movement that will positively impact millions of lives, but who knows? If living intentionally becomes a habit that you take with you through the stages of your life, if living consciously becomes a habit that you carry with you as you evolve, grow and become, and if living with greater awareness becomes a habit that you share with others throughout your life then you might be-the-cause or at least part of the cause and change the world.

Two images from *Star Trek the Next Generation* come to mind, when Captain Piccard says "make it so Number One" and "Engage". I will leave you with that challenge, since you are the next generation and we need all your positive energy to change the world.

Make it so Number One. Engage.

Bibliography

All scripture quotation - NIV

Chapter 1

Cornish, Edward, *The Study of the Future: An Introduction to the Art and Science of Understanding and Shaping Tomorrow's World*, 1977 World Future Society, Bethesda, MD.

Friedman, Thomas L., *The World is Flat: A Brief History of the Twenty-First Century.* 2007 Picador New York, NY

Wilcox, David, "Hold it Up to the Light" *Live Songs and Stories*, 2002 What Are Records?

Young, William P., *The Shack*, 2007 Windblown Media, Newberry Park, CA.

Chapter 2

Rohr, Richard, *Adam's Return: The Five Promises of Male Initiation.* 2004 Crossroads Publishing, New York, NY

Rohr, Richard, *From Wild Man to Wise Man: Reflections on Male Spirituality.* 2005 St. Anthony Messenger Press, Cincinnati, OH

Winner, Lauren F. *Mudhouse Sabbath: An Invitation to a Life of Spiritual Discipline.* 2003, Paraclete Press, Brewster Massachusetts.

Chapter 3

Creasy-Dean, Kenda & Foster, Ron, *The Godbearing Life: The Art of Soul Tending for Youth Ministry.* 1998, Upper Room Books, Nashville, Tennessee

Hersch, Patricia, *A Tribe Apart: A Journey into the Heart of American Adolescence.* 1998, Random House Publishing Group, New York, New York

Howard-Merritt, Carol, *Tribal Church: Ministering to the Missing Generation* 2007, Alban Institute, Herndon, Virginia

Oldenburg, Ray. *The Great Good Place: Cafes, Coffee Shops, Community Centers, Beauty Parlors, General Stores, Bars, Hangouts, and How They Get You Through the Day.* 1989, Paragon House, New York, New York

Tuckman, B, *Developmental sequence in small groups. Group Facilitation,* Spring 2001 *(3), 66-81*

Chapter 4 -

Carmichael, Alexader, *Carmina Gadelica: Hymns and Incantations Vol 1 &2.* 1900, Internet Version www.sacred-texts.com/neu/celt/cg1/index.htm

Newell, J. Phillip, *Listening for the Heartbeat of God: A Celtic Spirituality.* 1997, Paulist Press, Mahwah, New Jersey

Winner, Lauren F. *Mudhouse Sabbath: An Invitation to a Life of Spiritual Discipline.* 2003, Paraclete Press, Brewster Massachusetts.

Chapter 5 –

Robbins, Alexandra & Wilner, Abby. *Quaterlife Crisis: The Unique Challenges of Life in Your Twenties. 2001,* Jeremy P. Tarcher/Putnam, New York, New York.

Chapter 6 –

McLaren, Brian. *Presentation at Co-Creation Conference, 2012,* Servant Leadership School, Greensboro, NC

Postscript –

Rodenberry, Gene. *Star Trek: the Next Generation,* 1987-1994, Paramount Television, Los Angeles, California

Acknowledgements

Thanks to all the young adults who have let me walk this journey with them through the years. It has been my pleasure. I especially want to thank the students of Westminster Canterbury Fellowship at ASU. We go both ways! Thanks for letting me share try out all this on you folks through the years. Thanks to my Anam Cara – Bryan and Gavin. Thanks to my colleagues in campus ministry and in ministry with youth and young adults. Thanks to my sons Hayden and Shafer – you inspire me every day. Thanks to Parson's Porch Books. I am learning. Thanks again to my parents A.T. and Doris Brown for this life of ministry you launched me into. Camp is the greatest launching pad. Most of all thank you to my amazing, beautiful, gifted and challenging wife Karen. Thank you for your editing notes, your reading and re-reading, your patience, and especially for your love. Thanks you for all the years we have had and all the years to come. You are the best choice I ever made. I love you.

www.ingramcontent.com/pod-product-compliance
Lightning Source LLC
Chambersburg PA
CBHW070333090426
42733CB00012B/2467